# A CITY COMES OUT

# A CITY COMES OUT

### How Celebrities Made Palm Springs a
### Gay and Lesbian Paradise

## DAVID WALLACE

**BARRICADE**
**BOOKS**
FORT LEE, NEW JERSEY

Published by Barricade Books Inc.
185 Bridge Plaza North
Suite 308-A
Fort Lee, NJ 07024

www.barricadebooks.com

Library of Congress Cataloging-in-Publication Data
    Wallace, David.
    A city comes out : how celebrities made palm springs a gay and lesbian para-
dise / by David Wallace.
        p. cm.
    Includes bibliographical references and index.
    ISBN 978-1-56980-349-3 (hard cover : alk. paper)
  1. Gay men--California--Palm Springs--Biography. 2. Lesbians--California--
Palm Springs--Biography. 3. Gay men--California--Palm Springs--History. 4.
Lesbians--California--Palm Springs--History. 5. Gay community--California--
Palm Springs--History. 6. Palm Springs (Calif.)--History. I. Title.

    HQ75.7.W38 2008
    306.76'6092279497--dc22
    [B]
        2008022210

ISBN 13: 978-1-56980-349-3

10 9 8 7 6 5 4 3 2 1

Manufactured in the United States of America.

*This book is dedicated to the late Stephen Cross, my friend and neighbor, and a tragic victim of homophobia.*

# TABLE OF CONTENTS

# ACKNOWLEDGMENTS

Writing this book was helped immeasurably by the support of Carole Stuart, Ivy McFadden, Nick Mullandore, Jeri Vogelsang, Sally McManus, and the still lively ghosts of Hollywood who are so much a part of Palm Springs' history.

# INTRODUCTION

This is the story about a once dusty desert settlement that became the most famous gay and lesbian hometown and resort in America.

Some of it touches on those people who changed it by their actions…people like the late Gloria Greene, who was a pioneer in providing public places for gays and lesbians to gather and feel comfortable and then capping her life by co-establishing one of the area's most successful resources for AIDS victims.

Politicians are part of the story too, especially so in a city where the second mayor in a row and a majority of the city council are gay (at least at this writing). Gay architects and designers are reshaping the very look of the place via new commercial and residential developments as well as retirement communities especially designed for homosexual retirees. Businesses, straight and gay owned and operated, cater to the homosexual population as well as the thousands of gay and lesbian visitors celebrating the desert's sun, sex, and laid-back lifestyle; not to do so would be to risk financial disaster.

But for all that, Palm Springs, from its very beginnings, has been shaped by Hollywood. If one didn't know so on first arrival, then driving on the many streets named for stars (such as Dinah Shore Drive, Frank Sinatra Drive, and Gene Autry Trail) hammers home the point pretty effectively. Since the 1920s, Palm Springs has been a playground for Hollywood—both straight and gay—and escape to the desert was fairly easy, rarely more than a two-hour drive on the two-lane blacktops or a ride on the (much missed) trains of the day. It's about the same today unless freeway traffic is bad.

And it was natural for Hollywood's stars and power brokers to settle here after their careers faded...the place always has been fairly laid back and the weather—at least for seven or eight months of the year, was so damned nice. Since the film industry has always had a relatively high percentage of homosexual talent by its very nature it was inevitable that many of these new arrivals people were gay or lesbian, and thus by their very presence, they created both a uniquely hip image for the place and, despite occasional efforts of reactionary politicians and monied interests, an environment of tolerance.

First, a few words about the book.

Building a community is about people...the pioneers, the entrepreneurs, the politicians, the artists, the educators, and even the criminals. Put them all in a pot, mix them up over generations, and, for better or worse, you have a community. All this applies even more intensely in the evolution of Palm Springs into a world-famous gay and lesbian paradise, because many of the people who shaped the place—even if only by their presence— were, because of their Hollywood connections, among the best-known celebrities in the world in their time.

In their time.

The English romantic poet John Keats, who died of tuberculosis at twenty-five in 1821, requested that instead of bearing his name, his tombstone (in Rome's Protestant Cemetery) should read "Here lies one whose name was writ in water."

The evanescence of fame has been a matter of comment for millennia—Rome's philosopher-emperor Marcus Aurelius had something to say about it; so did Napoleon.

Nevertheless, it came as a shock to learn that a twenty-six-year-old friend, otherwise well educated, had never heard of Greta Garbo. Could it be that Garbo, once the most famous woman in the world and, until her death forty-nine years after making her last film (1941's *Two Faced Woman*), was a creature of hallowed mythology for millions (as well as being part of our story), is fading from our cultural consciousness? Apparently so.

That is why, for even the most famous characters in the homosexual saga of Palm Springs, I fill in some of their back stories—career and personal highlights, foibles, gossip and anecdotes about them, scandals, and triumphs. Much of this information was common knowledge (or commonly rumored) in their time—the warp and woof of who these people were—but at least in the memories of many readers, they may be fading into the shadows of the passing years.

Telling these stories also involves taking off rose-colored glasses while looking at the past.

Martin Scorsese once said, "When the legends start becoming reality, print the legends." I acknowledged his wry philosophy but mixed it with the facts behind the legends in writing my 2003 book about Hollywood's golden age traditions, *Hollywoodland*. But, because there are so many legends about many of the Hollywood stars who made Palm Springs famous as a gay and lesbian oasis—many of them the evolution of public relations blather of their era designed to disguise sexual orientation—I've reversed Scorsese's thinking while researching and writing this book: "When the reality starts becoming legend, print the reality" (or as much of it as one is able to discover). In some cases the results will possibly upset some readers brought up to believe that Hollywood propaganda was holy writ.

Also, as readers will also notice as they peruse the pages of this book, many of the gay, lesbian, and bisexual Palm Springs personalities were married—some even to straight partners—and some had children. This situation demands an explanation. Although they may have loved their spouses and certainly loved their children, these were marriages of convenience that were simply part of doing business in Hollywood at the time. And there was nothing new about such marriages, despite today's conservative assertions that all marriages have always been between a (straight) man and a (straight) woman.

Throughout history, marriages in which at least one of the members was a practicing homosexual have been more common than one might suspect, although, unlike the present demands for the legalization of same-sex unions, the reality behind such marriages was rarely talked about (but of course many people knew the truth).

Among the earliest recorded examples of such a marriage was that of the Greek orator and statesman Demosthenes (385–322 BC), who was known to have had many gay lovers although he was legally married. Even though Mary Queen of Scots' son King James I of England (who was also James VI of Scotland) and Anne of Denmark had eight children, court records of the time mention jealous rivalries between James' "male favorites," a code phrase for lovers. The most famous of them was George Villiers, whom James first made Earl and then Duke of Buckingham, and about whom the king famously wrote while, as a Christian, rather heretically implying something more: "You may be sure that I love the Earl of Buckingham more than anyone else…Jesus Christ did the same, and therefore I cannot be blamed. Christ had John, and I have George."

Also among such famous marriages was that of Oscar Wilde, who, some historians claim, had sex with more than a hundred young men but only one woman, with whom he fathered two children. Of course the famed playwright and poet eventually went to jail when his relationship with a young favorite, Lord Alfred Douglas (nicknamed "Bosie"), became a very public scandal.

Some writers have claimed that the marriage of Natacha Rambova and Rudolph Valentino in the early 1920s was unconsummated since both were gay or, in the case of Valentino, certainly bisexual. But this is an example of propaganda coming from the gay side, which also has to be understood and taken into account. The direct testimony of a friend and former roommate clearly indicates otherwise, as is seen in Chapter 2. Mercedes de Acosta, then a well-known married poet and playwright, was romantically linked with many famous lesbians of the Garbo era (including Garbo). Even such a highly visible relationship that might as well have been a marriage, like that between the young Cary Grant and Randolph Scott in the early 1930s, was tolerated if not completely accepted in Hollywood (at the time, the radio gossip commentator Jimmy Fiedler said of the Grant–Scott relationship: "These guys are carrying the buddy business a bit too far." Both went on to marriages, some, like Grant's, mostly unhappy; one, Scott's second union, lasted forty-three years.

But understanding and acceptance of such relationships within the film industry and letting the general public in on the facts were then (and to an extent even now) very different things. In much of America, the part that people occasionally dismiss today as "fly-over" country—places like Wichita, Omaha, and other cities, towns, and wide places in the road where the only entertainment may have been a weekend screening of the latest movie—most people had never heard the word "homosexual." And the term "gay" (derived from the French "gai" meaning high-spirited or merry) in its homosexual meaning didn't become part of the vernacular until the late 1960s, although it had been in use as self-reference among homosexuals since the 1920s. Those millions of ticket buyers in America and the rest of the world were the last people that the studios wanted to learn that the latest matinee idol preferred men as sexual partners rather than women, and that the hottest leading lady liked ladies.

Then a major gay scandal exploded. In 1933 William Haines, a name unfamiliar to most people these days but at that time one of the most popular actors in the country, was caught having sex with a man and was immediately fired (the story is related in Chapter 13).

This was just the latest of a growing list of Hollywood scandals, including the 1923 death of another leading man, Wallace Reid, by a drug overdose, the arrest and trials of Roscoe "Fatty" Arbuckle for bringing about the death of a popular Hollywood starlet (he was acquitted after three trials but his career was ruined), and the 1922 murder of William Desmond Taylor, a famous director rumored to be having a clandestine gay relationship with his chauffeur as well as a straight relationship with Mary Miles Minter, one of the most famous silent stars.

The industry reacted by installing a self-censor and then, in 1934, a production code. Eventually it realized it had to do more; it toughened the code and required all films to obtain a certificate of approval before release. Among the casualties of such censorship was the double bed...it was sleeping solo on the silver screen from then on for more than a generation, and of course any reference to homosexuality as well as the ridicule of religion was expressly banned. The new rule would precipitate the end of the career of Mae West, famous for her sexual double entendres, and would radically change the films.

The newly toughened censorship bureau (it was formally known as the Production Code Administration but everyone called it the Breen Code after its head, a notoriously conservative and anti-Semitic Roman Catholic named Joseph Breen). The tighter rules also demanded that the studios make sure their stars never strayed from the (literally) straight and narrow path by forcing them to insert morality clauses into their contracts.

Under studio pressure, Cary Grant (see Chapter 4) quickly married (he would remarry four more times and father a daughter, despite bouts of depression and at least one attempted suicide). Randolph Scott also got married soon thereafter, but the pair—with and without their wives—lived more or less together for years afterward. Wedding bells began ringing all over Hollywood as homosexual and bisexual stars sought refuge in marriages of convenience to protect their public reputations and thus preserve their careers. Such arrangements were called "lavender marriages" by Hollywood insiders and the tabloid press, but rarely so by the mainline media or the general public.

•••••

Despite being married three times, Sir Laurence Olivier, one of the greatest actors of the twentieth century, was a far from conventional husband. Celebrity biographer Axel Madsen described his first marriage to actress Jill Esmond as "a sham," adding that Esmond was a member of "the sewing circle," the then-popular term for the powerful group of lesbian and bisexual women in theater and films. After his divorce from Esmond, Olivier wed Vivien Leigh and also became the lover of comic actor Danny Kaye, whose marriage to composer Sylvia Fine was probably purely professional. According to author

Donald Spoto, Leigh "constantly upbraided" Olivier about his affair with Kaye; but it was his third wife, Joan Plowright, who finally forced the actor to end the ten-year gay relationship.

The Hollywood censor is gone (so are those single beds), but over the decades many famous stars have tied the knot under suspicious circumstances. Barbara Stanwyck was rumored to have had affairs with both Marlene Dietrich and Joan Crawford (and others) when she married Robert Taylor, who was plagued by gay rumors of his own. Judy Garland's marriage to director Vincente Minnelli was rumored to be a cover for Minnelli's homosexuality. Charles Laughton and Elsa Lanchester's marriage was famously lavender, and, while living with faithful companions, Katherine Hepburn (Chapter 6), famous for playing near-androgynous parts like 1935's *Sylvia Scarlett*—maintained a studio-approved image even in Palm Springs, where she often escaped with the alcoholic Spencer Tracy (who never divorced his wife) and apparently, as we will see, also indulged her lesbian leanings.

Psycho star Tony Perkins and Berry Berenson maintained the façade of a happy family, complete with two children and a long-running marriage, despite the fact that, as Tab Hunter revealed in his 2003 tell-all memoir, *Tab Hunter, Confidential*, he and Perkins had been lovers for years. And perhaps the most famous case of a lavender marriage was that of Tab Hunter's famous contemporary, Rock Hudson (Chapter 7), who succumbed to pressure from his studio (and threats that a tabloid magazine was planning to expose his homosexuality) and married his agent's secretary, Phyllis Gates, at the height of his stardom in 1955.

As we will see, often the relationships of some of the couples in the book can be as complex as a Jackson Pollock painting; the choices of sexual partners by a person such as Janet Gaynor can seem positively kaleidoscopic—at first glance. And of course, just like in heterosexual society, it takes all types to tango, and that has always been as true in Palm Springs as anywhere else...

populated by gays who flaunt it (like Truman Capote) as well as those, like Tab Hunter, who believe that what one does in the bedroom should stay in the bedroom (well, other than writing a best-selling book about it; but it did take him more than four decades to do so).

And that's what makes the gay and lesbian history of Palm Springs as engrossing as a Hitchcock whodunit.

# CHAPTER ONE

# PALM SPRINGS TODAY

I n recent years Palm Springs, California, has become famous as probably the most popular gay and lesbian resort in the nation.

The reason? Well, certainly a major cause for Palm Springs' fame as a homosexual heaven is the White Party, held every spring since 1989, when some 20,000 gay men descend on the community for what is billed by its promoters as "the nation's largest gay dance festival." The event is also Palm Springs' biggest moneymaker...contributing (in 2007, according to the city controller) more than $4 million to the city's economy plus millions more to neighboring communities.

•••••

Frequently coinciding with the White Party is the Dinah Shore (golf) weekend, now known as the LPGA Nabisco Tournament and headquartered in nearby Rancho Mirage. Founded in 1972, it regularly attracts thousands of lesbians from around the world.

But the city is also far more than a gay and lesbian resort. Even without the spring events, it is in fact, as Mayor Steven Pougnet (who is gay) says, "the preeminent gay city in America."

San Francisco and New York would certainly win that designation on the basis of sheer numbers of gay and lesbian residents. But as a percentage of the total population, Palm Springs wins hands down, with a permanent homosexual population estimated to be over 40 percent. That's more than eight times the estimated national average and some three or four times the gay and lesbian percentage of San Francisco, often cited as the "gayest" city in America.

Such a huge gay and lesbian presence affects everything: gay-owned businesses are flourishing and there are dozens of gay and lesbian resorts in Palm Springs and neighboring communities. The White Party, for example, is headquartered at the mainline Wyndham Hotel, where, on the party weekend, hundreds of gay men in various stages of undress frolic in the pool. It's certainly a sight that's the last thing ex-major Frank Bogert and the late president Gerald Ford, both very establishment, straight men, could have imagined when they dedicated the hotel in April 1986.

The city's gayness has also caused a near tectonic shift in the city's politics, after generations of civic leadership by an "old boys' club" of conservative, straight, white males such as Bogert. (Sonny Bono, mayor from 1988 to 1992, was an exception; although white and straight, he was more gay- and lesbian-friendly than his predecessors or his successor, William Kleindienst.) And it was the gay and lesbian reaction to Kleindienst's perceived ambivalence toward the homosexual community to which many attribute both the 2003 election of Ron Oden, Palm Springs' first gay mayor (and the nation's first black gay mayor), and a gay majority on the city council.

Steven Pougnet, forty-six, elected to succeed Oden in 2007

with an astonishing 71 percent of the vote, was actually the first openly gay politician to be elected in the city when he ran for city council in that 2003 election that would dramatically change things at Palm Springs' City Hall (Oden came out while in office; Ginny Foat, a lesbian city council member, was at first appointed to the city council and was later elected, in 2005).

According to Pougnet, by the time he ran for mayor, even such old-guard organizations as the local newspaper, the *Desert Sun* (owned by the conservative Gannett Newspaper chain), had moved from acceptance of the city's gay and lesbian readership to support. "I was the first gay politician they ever endorsed," Pougnet laughs, "and as far as I can tell, the first Democrat. When I met with the paper's editorial board before my election I was asked what I considered had the biggest impact of anything I had done in my life. I told them it was when they changed their policy and printed the news of my civil union with my partner in the newspaper [Pougnet and his partner, Christopher Green, were married in Vermont in 2002]. The *New York Times* had only begun printing news of same-sex unions about then."

•••••

In their endorsement, the newspaper also saluted a talent of Pougnet's of which he is especially proud: his ability to achieve consensus between opposing viewpoints. The *Desert Sun*'s also believed that his background would best qualify him "to help guide Palm Springs in being the type of city that will continue to attract tourism while protecting the quality of life residents crave." Note: not a word of his being gay.

Pougnet and Green's hitherto unorthodox lifestyle was, however, widely noted when it was announced in April 2006 that he and Christopher had become parents of biological children, a boy and a girl, named Beckham and Julia (by separate surrogate mothers; Beckham is two minutes older than his sister). "They are certainly the poster boys of the new Palm Springs," says local architect Doug Hudson, designer of Port Lawrence, the planned mixed-use development deliberately designed to attract residents (and new retail businesses) to the city's downtown area.

Rick Hutcheson, a gay member of Palm Springs' City Council, was also endorsed by the *Desert Sun* when he ran for election in 2007. He explains how he and his partner ended up in the city: "We met when we both came to Palm Springs to enjoy a very gay-friendly resort after spending Christmas with our respective families," Hutcheson says. "Then, after dating cross-country for about half a year, we bought a home here." That home, initially planned as a weekend escape, quickly became something much more. "We found that we were living in Palm Springs and commuting to our work out of town," Hutcheson says (strenuous, but perhaps less so than longtime Palm Springs resident Barry Manilow, who commutes daily to Nevada for his Las Vegas Hilton show). Eventually they developed what is a mini-real estate empire in the city where they now live full-time.

"Palm Springs is, as everyone who sees it knows, a beautiful part of the world," Hutcheson adds. "Every time of the day here you get a different vista and a different set of colors; it's also an easy place to live and, for a gay couple, it's very welcoming. But I think the friendliness of Palm Springs is not an 'in your face friendliness,' it's just a comfortableness. I believe it's part of what's going on nationally in relations between gay people and straight people. [Being gay] is not such a big deal anymore in Palm Springs as well as most other places in the country... there is less and less fuss about it. For many of the younger generation, 'coming out' is an archaic term.

"And," he adds, "just because there is a gay majority of the city council, there is no 'gay agenda.' We deal with the same sort of problems all city governments confront—fixing our streets, dealing with break-ins, reviving our downtown area. Despite the large gay presence here, people get along just like [straight] people in other places…they're just your neighbors, the people you work with, your customers, and so on."

"My partner, Erich Burkhart, and I started coming as tourists around 1980," says Doug Hudson, who, in addition to designing the city's dramatic new Port Lawrence development, has also designed a number of homes, which, like his own, represent a dramatic departure both from Palm Springs' early twentieth-century Spanish Revival architecture and from the iconic mid-century homes that to many define the built environment of the place. (This image of Palm Springs as a midcentury architectural mecca was certainly enhanced by the publicity surrounding the auction in May 2008 of the home Richard Neutra designed for Edgar Kaufmann in 1946 marketed by Christie's auction house as a piece of art rather than a house.)

"The weather, of course, is beautiful…when it's gloomy in L.A. it can be sunny and nice here," Hudson says. "When we began coming out here, Erich's parents had a mobile home out in Desert Hot Springs, a community several miles north of Palm Springs, and it was a great place to stay for young guys who were working hard.

"And it was only two hours from L.A. and there were some gay bars [then only in nearby Cathedral City], so we could go out," he says. "There were only a couple gay hotels but we obviously didn't have to go there.

"Moving here was a gradual process," Hudson recalls. "Ten years ago we decided we wanted a weekend place here. We knew we wanted to be in the Las Palmas neighborhood [from the early days, Las Palmas was Palm Springs' premier neighborhood, once home to directors such as Jack Warner and later even Elvis Presley and Liberace], and when we started looking it was before the huge explosion of prices here. Now," he laughs, "we keep think-ing: 'could of, would of, should of.'"

Hudson and his partner's move to Palm Springs is a pro-cess shared by many full-time residents. "In 2000 we found the property we ended up buying," Hudson adds, "perfect for us, an older house on a big piece of land on a good street with a great postcard view of the mountain framed by palm trees." Because remodeling the older house turned out to be as expensive as building a new one, the pair decided to opt for the new. "Then, going back to Los Angeles every Sunday evening [they also have a home in Beverly Hills] became very frustrating," Doug adds. "I was beginning to be more involved in Palm Springs...I became a member of the city's architectural advisory commit-tee and then joined the board of the Palm Springs Preservation Foundation...both mainstream organizations as well as support-ing gay-oriented charities like the AIDS Assistance Program." (The AAP feeds hundreds of local HIV/AIDS programs; it was cofounded by the city's late hostess Gloria Greene, Chapter 15.)

Despite Palm Springs' social advances, Hudson and Burkhart still find pockets of resentment, but "not at all" because they are gay. "We're a part of a 'new generation,'" Hudson says, "and a lot of old-timers here in town, the good old boys, still have quite a bit of resentment toward newcomers, carpetbaggers, coming into town and stealing part of their thunder. The old boys are still in power in some professions."

•••••

So what was it that made Palm Springs uniquely qualified to become America's homosexual heaven?

"Palm Springs has," Hudson says, taking a broader view, "the natural beauty, the weather, the history, but most important it

has the geographic location close to Los Angeles and an airport.
It has all the pieces in place that make it a new kind of city: the
balance of leisure activities, art, lifestyle, a great new conven-
tion center [site of the White Party's biggest weekend event],
hotels and more to come, fine restaurants, a [Native American–
owned] casino, and professional opportunities. I've often used
the example of Miami Beach, which was 'rediscovered' in the
1980s…it takes a while, but when the pieces are all in place, as is
said: 'Build it and they will come.'"

By way of explaining the success of the White Party (which
was a success from the beginning despite efforts by past city
fathers to halt it), producer Jeffrey Sanker also agrees with Hudson on what is probably the main historic as well as contemporary reason for Palm Springs' popularity with both gay and
straight vacationers as well as permanent residents: "One of the
big things has to be the location. Palm Springs is a truly magical place," Sanker says. "The desert is warm and the scenery is
magnificent." He adds: "The White Party has really become sort
of a tradition for a large number of guys. It's like one big, happy
reunion every year, a celebration of camaraderie like none other
that I've ever seen."

Jade Nelson, a thirty-two-year-old Palm Springs native,
echoes Sanker's conviction that a great part of Palm Springs'
attraction for gay men (and lesbians as well) is the atmosphere
of freedom to be oneself. "I knew I was gay from an early age,"
Nelson says, "but I didn't feel comfortable here because, at the
time, I thought it [being gay] was an old man thing…I rarely
saw any young gay men.

"Then, one day during Spring Break in 1995, I was driving
down Avenida Caballeros at 5:30 A.M. to my job as a pastry chef
at Smoke Tree Ranch [a family-oriented local resort since the
1930s], and suddenly there were all these half-naked men running across the street." Although such displays are still deplored

by many residents, the experience was, for Nelson, liberating. "I realized this was one of the few places in the country where gay men could assemble peaceably and have a weekend of pure, uninterrupted celebration."

In 2002, after working in Seattle, Nelson returned to a Palm Springs that was even more dramatically changed from that of his childhood. "There were gay couples everywhere," he says, "walking down the street holding hands, and buying houses." Today the Palm Springs High School, where Jade encountered a wall of homophobia in the early 1990s, now has an open membership club named the Gay/Straight Alliance, which draws between fifteen and forty-five students to its weekly meetings.

For some, one aspect of the city's tolerance has been carried too far with the presence of some three dozen "clothing-optional" resorts centered in the Warm Sands neighborhood. But whether or not you approve of the concept, of clothing-optional resorts, their presence is an early example of the power of gay entrepreneurship in Palm Springs.

They came about largely because of one of the factors Sanker cites as a cause for the success of the White Party, and that has also been, historically, the resort's leading attraction: the weather.

•••••

The first business to open in Palm Springs after the first non-Indian settled in the area in 1883 was a place for visitors to stay. More accurately, it was a sanatorium where victims of tuberculosis could come to recover. In fact, the original Desert Inn, which was built in 1909 and later would become a famed resort catering to the very wealthy, including the Vanderbilts and Hearsts as well as Hollywood celebrities, also began as a tuberculosis sanatorium. (Las Vegas' Desert Inn started in 1946 and was modeled after the long-gone Palm Springs resort, which was located downtown where the Desert Fashion Plaza has stood vacant for some time).

By the 1930s and 1940s a number of vacation bungalows as well as the newly coined "motels" sprang up in the Warm Sands area, catering to vacationers who didn't demand (or care for) the facilities of a full resort like the Desert Inn or the then equally celebrated El Mirador. The Desert Inn made much of the fact that Shirley Temple often stayed there with her family, but they earlier stayed at what is now the clothing-optional Warm Sands Villas.

Most locals agree that Palm Springs had begun to come out of the closet in 1976 when El Mirasol, a small resort Howard Hughes built for his friends on Warm Sands Drive in 1947 (and where he reportedly stashed his mistresses as well as friends), was converted into a gay resort. This was followed by more and more such operations. In 1984 Bob Mellen, who has been waggishly described as "the mayor of Warm Sands," opened what was apparently the first of the local clothing-optional resorts, the Vista Grande (he and his partner, Robert Fields, now own four such resorts).

Because of a more lenient environment, the prototype of today's gay resorts was in the nearby and more easygoing Cathedral City. Originally a 2.5-acre Elizabeth Arden "beauty farm," it was also a historic property with a restaurant housed in an adobe building dating back to the early 1800s when the place was a Pony Express stop. The resort's then-famous date palms stood throughout the hotel's evolution, first as a lesbian resort in the 1970s and later as a gay resort called Dave's Villa Capri. With its "outdoor bathhouse," "it was the wildest place on the planet," Mellen laughs, "and it inspired the resorts in Warm Sands." (Remodeled and renamed simply as The Villa, it had a shorter life, closing in 2007.) Because of its more relaxed policies, Cathedral

City was also the site of most of the Coachella Valley's first gay and lesbian bars including the Gaf—"fag" spelled backward—and Gloria Greene's popular His & Hers.

Besides the weather, another main reason for Palm Springs' early popularity as a gay and lesbian (and straight) destination is its proximity to Los Angeles. From the top stars to lowly studio employees, for generations the place has provided an escape from the pressures of the film capital, which, although the fact was largely accepted but little discussed, has had a large gay and lesbian population since the early days of the movie industry itself.

"And, don't forget, Palm Springs has always been about having fun," says Robert Fields; it was not necessary for him to add that much of that "fun," of course—gay or straight—often involved sex (and still does). "Also many gay men like taking their clothes off," says John Turk, owner of South Pasadena's Mission Antiques who, with his partner, Jim Maier, an ex-Jesuit priest, vacations annually at one of the city's clothing-optional gay resorts.

What really cemented Palm Springs' standing as a gay and lesbian haven from the beginning, at least according to the Reverand Andrew Green, longtime (straight) rector of St. Paul in the Desert Episcopal Church, which boasts a large gay membership, was privacy provided by a crucial aspect of Palm Springs' original built environment: its walls. Walls around homes, walls around resorts and hotels, walls, seemingly, once around everything, thus offering privacy from prying eyes for gay and lesbian activities ranging from informal social gatherings to simply soaking up some rays around a glittering pool, to "having fun."

"I first came to Palm Springs when I was invited to a party in 1980," recalls a local businessman, then twenty-three, who requested anonymity to protect his La Quinta business (about twenty miles down-valley from Palm Springs), where he still encounters homophobia. (Although Palm Springs is obviously very liberal today, the towns "down-valley," among them Rancho Mirage and La Quinta, "get redder and redder" says the editor of a local magazine.) "I had never seen so many beautiful men and women," he adds. "I came back a second weekend and never left.

"Palm Springs wasn't overtly gay then," he adds. "Everything happened inside walls and gates," he says, confirming Rev. Green's judgment. "Everything was very private. There wasn't much public gay life."

When the growing popularity of Palm Springs as a gay resort met the plummeting real estate values of the early 1980s (caused in part by a misguided "no-growth" policy, which midwifed nearby Palm Desert's commercial boom), the transformation exploded.

Architecture connoisseurs, many of them gay and lesbian, quickly discovered they could buy a classic, midcentury house for next to nothing, especially the tract homes built by the Alexander Construction Company from the early 1950s until the mid-1960s, many sporting the designer's unusual "butterfly" roofs. Today surviving examples of the 2,000 or so Alexanders, which cost an average of $25,000 when new, can sell for over a million dollars (restored, of course; the originals had little or no insulation since they were intended as winter homes only).

And the attractions was not limited to inexpensive classic houses. "It wasn't long before people realized that the [Warm Sands] neighborhood which had once been a destination for vacationing families," Mellen says, "was a potential gold mine for exclusively male clothing-optional resorts." In the beginning some of the clothing-optional resorts were mixed, but women soon gravitated to lesbian motels and hotels. Among the first was The Desert Knight, established in 1969 by Eadie Adams and her partner, Pat McGrath, which, according to Howard Johns in *Palm Springs Confidential*, numbered Gloria Swanson among its guests. It has been renamed the Queen of Hearts Resort.

As a dramatic commentary on the evolution of Palm Springs into today's more tolerant community, when El Mirasol was converted into a gay resort, six-foot walls were added to enclose each unit's private patio. They were cut down to fence height in 2000 by the present owners.

"When [the late] Gloria Greene, who owned His & Hers bar in Cathedral City, opened Gloria's restaurant and bar in the early 1980s, she really brought gay life in Palm Springs to life," Mellen says. First located downtown and later on North Palm Canyon Drive, the place became so popular that on the day that Reverend Green first arrived at his parish in 1990, it was to Gloria's that he was taken to lunch by a member of his new congregation. Then, with the opening in 1991 of the Street Bar Named Desire, the first solely gay bar in the city, Palm Springs' public gay and lesbian social scene was on its way.

Although it has taken only a relatively short time for all this to happen, so much has changed that it seems far longer.

Just consider one example: The community's acceptance of Mayor Pougnet's very public lifestyle as well as support for his political ambitions has occurred little more than a generation after a previous rector of St. Paul in the Desert was literally hounded out of town when it was discovered that he was gay.

Today the city, primarily through its dramatic acceptance of the gay and lesbian lifestyles, has evolved in seemingly no time at all from what was once—on the surface, anyway—a conservative, Republican, winter family resort into a community where people of diverse ethnicities, philosophies, lifestyles, and sexual preferences are not only accepted but celebrated. Perhaps the place actually has become, as many suggest these days, a model for the twenty-first-century city.

How that came about is our story.

# CHAPTER TWO

# FLORILLA AND ROSE AND
# RUDY AND NATACHA

he Palm Springs area has been inhabited for more than 500 years by what was then—and is now—a relatively small band of Cahuilla Indians. Today, in fact, the Indians have become major players in the city, masters (for that is what "Cahuilla" means in their native tongue) of not only the nearby, picturesque canyons but also the hugely successful Palm Springs Casino and Spa (a favorite of both straight and gay residents and tourists).

Only a century ago, however, the Cahuillas were basically living off the land in the oasis below the soaring, 10,804-foot Mount San Jacinto, which they considered a sacred mountain and the home of the evil demon Tahquitz (today memorialized by a canyon and a major thoroughfare in the city). "A brave, rugged, lot of aborigines," George Wharton James romanticized in his appropriately titled 1914 book *California, Romantic and Beautiful*. "They used the wonderful…spring at Palm Springs (Agua Caliente) as their health resort, gathering their big-pitted dates from the palms of Palm Canyon, collecting their acorns from the mountain slopes, and making their mush, flour, bread, tortillas, drink, and candy from the beans found on the mesquite trees which dotted the desert's face on either side."

However idealized, that lifestyle was changing, first from the pressure of the railroad, which came through the valley in 1876, and, far more influential, from the huge success of a novel written in 1884 by Helen Hunt Jackson, once an Indian agent in the area. The novel was *Ramona*, memorialized by the names of countless streets and businesses throughout Southern California as well as by the Ramona Pageant, a theatrical adaptation of the novel presented since 1923 in the community of Hemet in the mountains near Palm Springs. The event is said to be the largest outdoor festival in the country. The story's hero, Alessandro, was patterned on a real Cahuilla Indian named Juan Diego, and Ramona, herself, was also a Cahuilla whose full name was Ramona Lubo; they are, in fact, buried next to each other in the old Cahuilla cemetery in the mountains.

So, you might well ask, where is all this leading? Directly to the rather amazing fact that Palm Springs—the Palm Springs that grew into a thriving desert community and world-famous resort—got its start (actually a restart after a decade-long drought nearly killed off the original agricultural community that was laid out after the first non-Indian families settled there around the turn of the twentieth century) largely because of the work of a number of dedicated women, some of whom almost certainly were lesbian.

At least one of these pioneering women was the community's first doctor and, if circumstantial evidence is to be believed, was one of the earliest lesbian residents: Florilla White.

Circumstantial evidence, however, is about all one has to go on, since a century ago lesbianism was carried on behind tightly closed doors. Lesbian love was beyond mention; in fact the word wasn't even used; one reason being that when Palm Springs was in its infancy, only one in a thousand people knew that such relationships did or even could exist. The knowledge of a male homosexual subculture was better known, thanks in part to the playwright Oscar Wilde (1854–1900), whose flamboyance often brought ridicule (not unlike right-wing media today in reporting the frequently flamboyant Gay Pride parades and festivals). Nevertheless, gayness—despite its prevalence—was also a banned subject within "polite" society of the time. King Edward VII, who reigned from 1901 until his death in 1910, refused to believe that his oldest son, Albert Victor (actually named by the king's domineering mother, Queen Victoria, to memorialize herself and her beloved late consort, Prince Albert; the young prince was known as "Eddy") was almost certainly gay despite undeniable proof that he patronized gay brothels. When Albert died of pneumonia in 1892 at the age of twenty-eight, the establishment breathed a sigh of relief, openly commenting on their escape from having a homosexual king. As an example of a particularly malicious form of gay-bashing, some recent authors have even suggested that "Eddy" was the notorious Jack the Ripper, despite court records that prove he wasn't anywhere near London at the time of the murders.

So, considering the era when Florilla White lived in Palm Springs (she first arrived in 1912), it's understandable that any lesbianism was very closeted. Somewhat perplexing is why today, in these relatively emancipated times, especially in Palm Springs, the possibility that she may have been a lesbian is still passionately denied by some, albeit members of the city's once-reigning, straight, "aristocracy."

But consider the following: According to the Palm Springs Historical Society, it has been revealed in a scholarly thesis by New Mexico Highlands University graduate student Jessica Levis that a wealthy woman named Rose Dougan lived in Palm Springs—or at least spent long vacations in the growing resort community—beginning in the 1930s.

In a town the size of Palm Springs at the time (the population was around 3,000) it was perhaps inevitable that Dr. White and Dougan met. One source claims they may have "co-habited" for some of those years. They did. A recent search of the local records proves not only that Dougan was living in Palm Springs in 1938 (her house was located where the present Moortens Botanical Garden is on South Palm Canyon), but during 1941 and 1942—the year Dr. White died—they shared the same address. Dougan remained in the city until 1957, living in a house she owned not far from her first residence.

And there is no question in that Dougan (or Doougan as her name is occasionally spelled) was a relatively "out" lesbian despite the attitude of the time. She first turned up in the mid-teens when she and her lover, the Baroness Vera (or Verra) von Blumenthal (of minor Russian nobility who fled the revolution) arrived in Santa Fe, New Mexico.

Dougan, apparently originally from Indiana or Illinois, was one of the first female pilots; she was said to have been taught to fly by one of the Wright Brothers at the Huffman Prairie flying field where they developed their flying machines. It is part of Santa Fe's lore that the first plane to fly over the state capital was piloted by Dougan with von Blumenthal as a passenger. She was also one of the first people to take the local Pueblo pottery seriously. In 1918 Dougan and von Blumenthal built a home, named "Duchess Castle," and a school northwest of Santa Fe in what is now Bandelier State Park, and they set out both to teach more local Indians how to make pottery and, at the same time, to develop its credibility as an art form.

The couple succeeded more than they could ever have dreamed.

The house and school are today in ruins, but the production and sale of Pueblo Indian pottery is a huge business today, as anyone who prices an old Indian pot well knows. The couple also got an archeologist named Edgar Lee Hewitt and his assistant,

Kenneth Chapman, excited over Indian art and artifacts, and together they founded the Indian Fair Committee. Designed both
to provide an outlet for the Indians' work and to reward excel-
lence through a prize competition, it was the direct ancestor of
today's Santa Fe Indian Market, a world famous event held every
August. Dougan also provided funds to the Museum of New
Mexico to collect and promote Indian art; in 1922 a Hopi named
Kabotie won the first annual Rose Dougan art prize, and by 1930
his works were in the museum's permanent collection.

Dougan and von Blumenthal's evangelism for Indian art and
crafts is also credited with influencing today's famous Santa Fe
"Adobe Central" appearance. Until the 1920s, much of Santa Fe
looked much like any other wood-frame, wood-sidewalk Western town, although there were plenty of adobe buildings and
houses. But when all the hoopla over Indian art and culture began attracting artists such as Georgia O'Keeffe, the town soon
began to adobe-ize everything.

Dougan's health was apparently never good, and eventually
the couple began summering at their place near Santa Fe and
spending the winter in Pasadena. There von Blumenthal, hoping
to promote Russian handicrafts in the United States, founded the
(short-lived) Russian Peasant Handicraft Center, which boasted
an adjoining tearoom complete with bubbling samovars of tea.
(In a somewhat weird confluence of popular culture and history,
the television series *Northern Exposure* was set in a town founded
by an artistically inclined lesbian couple, one of whom was sickly.)
And it seems that some, perhaps many, of those winters also
were spent visiting Dr. White and living in Palm Springs.

•••••

Dr. White was also a close friend of a legendary actor who was
probably gay (at least clearly bisexual) and his second wife, her-

self certainly bisexual but probably a lesbian who was the protégé of the most famous lesbian actresses in Hollywood. But
more about that a little bit on.

First, a little more about Palm Springs' beginnings, since Dr.
White was so much a part of it.

The community that would be Palm Springs was born in
1884 when John McCallum and his family, seeking a warm, dry
climate that would be healthier for his son, who suffered from
tuberculosis, became the first permanent non-Indian residents
of Palm City, as it was then called. Within a year he opened
the area's first store and soon constructed miles of rock-lined
irrigation canals to bring water from the nearby canyons to a
320-acre property he and his partners decided to develop as an
agricultural community (now downtown Palm Springs). Exactly
a decade later, following a year when there was so much rain
that McCallum's irrigation ditches were washed out, there was
a devastating, eleven-year drought, during which McCallum,
his tubercular son, and two other sons (and shortly thereafter a
daughter) died.

During that drought a Scotsman, Welwood Murray, arrived
and settled in the tiny community. Knowing that the drought
would end one day, and realizing that there were no facilities
for people to stay in the tiny community, he built the area's first
hotel, appropriately named the Palm Springs Hotel.

Cut ahead twenty years or so. The dedicated women mentioned earlier, who were then called "angels in skirts," began to
arrive in force in the hitherto male-dominated village. ("Angels
in skirts," typical of the sentimental terminology of the time,
was a bit too poetic since many of them adopted garb more ap-
propriate to the city's climate and rusticity and never wore skirts
again.)

In the winter of 1912 Florilla White, born into a Utica, New
York, farming family in 1871, visited Palm Springs and stayed

at Murray's hotel. The following year she and her younger sister, Cornelia, returned, and they bought and operated Murray's Palm Springs Hotel. Cornelia, by the way, was quite an adventurer for her time, and there are more than a few people who believe she was also a lesbian (again, such a possibility is vehemently denied today by some older residents of Palm Springs). When Cornelia was twenty, she spent a year—unchaperoned—in Europe. She later explored above the Arctic Circle, sailed up the Nile, and taught practical courses in plumbing and carpentry at the University of North Dakota before becoming a banana and papaya farmer in tropical Mexico until she, along with Florilla, was forced to dramatically escape the 1912 revolution on a hand-pumped railroad hand car.

When they acquired the Palm Springs Hotel, it was one of only fifteen commercial buildings in the entire village. Florilla, besides being a medical doctor, was also a passionate horsewoman and nature lover and would often spend days in the mountains, at least until she became the village's health officer during World War I.

And there things stood until, after the war, Hollywood discovered that the desert around Palm Springs was the perfect location for filming the escapist adventure films popular then (and now, for that matter). And among them were some of the movies that would make a twenty-six-year-old Italian immigrant named Rodolpho Alfonso Raffaelo Filiberto Guglielmi di Valentina d'Antonguolla the most famous male actor in the world. Rudolph Valentino—for that is how he became known—came to America in 1913 and lived in New York, working as a waiter, a gardener, and a professional dancer—he once stood in for the famously gay Clifton Webb, who would himself later find fame in Hollywood but nothing to match that of the younger dancer. Valentino was often so poor that he slept in a then far safer Central Park.

All this would change when a friend—who may have been a customer, since Valentino was said to be picking up spending money as a male hustler—was struck by the handsome youth's appearance and suggested that he go into movies. Valentino hopped the first train west, which also happened to be the train carrying the cast and company of the Broadway show *The Passing Crowd* to Los Angeles; its star, Al Jolson, would, less than a decade later, become the first famous voice of sound films.

It was not as an actor but mostly as a dancer that Valentino got his first work in Hollywood, first as an uncredited performer but by 1918 under various versions of his own name. That year he made *The Married Virgin*, for which he was paid fifty dollars, the same amount that he was given for dancing in a later film, *The Rogue's Romance*, for which his fee was based on the film footage shot of him: a dollar a foot.

Valentino's troubles with women started early on.

At a party in 1919 he met a scenario writer named Jean Acker whom he married on November 5, 1919. (A scenario writer wrote the story of a film in those silent movie days as well as the cards with a sentence or two written on them that carried the otherwise mimed action forward.) Since Acker was well known to be a lesbian, the young actor must have seen the union solely as a career move; she was well connected in the film community and was making a good income ($200 weekly, the equivalent of $2,500 or more today). Nevertheless, he had to have been surprised when, after the wedding, the couple went to Acker's room at the Hotel Hollywood—Valentino had to produce a copy of the wedding license before the desk clerk would allow him to go upstairs—and she slammed and locked the door in Valentino's face, wailing that she had made a terrible mistake. That was the end of the great "Latin Lover's" first marriage, although the couple wouldn't divorce for three years. Later Valentino, by then the most famous actor in the world and making $200,000 plus 50 percent of the profits per film, blamed the failure of his marriage on her greed ("Jean always claimed that she wanted to be my soul mate, but what she really wanted was to be my check-mate"). The real reason for such an excuse was his clear realization that in the public's mind, no "real man" would marry a lesbian, and to admit he was gay or bisexual would then spell death for his career.

In May 1922, soon after the release of his film *The Sheik* made him a star and just months before *The Four Horsemen of the Apocalypse* would make him the most famous male movie star in the world, Valentino married Natacha Rambova. She was a lesbian who was the costume designer on the 1921 film *Camille*, in which Valentino co-starred with the legendary Alla Nazimova (famously lesbian and the person who also created golden age Hollywood's naughtiest hotel, the Garden of Allah; she later became Nancy Reagan's godmother). Despite her Russian-sounding name, Rambova was an American, born in Salt Lake City in January 1897 and christened Winifred Kimball Shaughnessy; she was the daughter of a former federal marshal and mining entrepreneur and his wife, a descendant of a Mormon patriarch. She was also the stepniece of Elsie de Wolfe, the woman generally credited as the founder of interior decorating, and she spent many vacations at de Wolfe's celebrated home in Versailles, France.

In 1915 Shaughnessy joined the Theodore Kosloff dance studio in Los Angeles, assumed her new name, and designed the costumes for Kosloff's grandly titled Imperial Russian Ballet when it toured America the following year. She also began designing sets and costumes for the fledgling film industry and was an intimate friend of Nazimova, who got her the costume job on *Camille*.

Apparently the couple were instantly attracted to each other despite Rambova's lesbianism. Despite stories that the union was unconsummated, cameraman Paul Ivano, a friend with whom the couple shared a flat at Hollywood's old Formosa Apartments, claimed that they made love "like tigers."

Ivano specifically recalled one night when he was awakened by a naked, still erect Valentino screaming that he had "killed Natacha." She wasn't dead, just passed out from their vigorous lovemaking, and Ivano eventually revived Rambova by sponging her naked body (he also told Valentino to stay away until she cooled down).

In some ways, theirs was a perfect relationship—at least in the beginning. Valentino needed her common sense to help run his career, and she loved his physicality ("Rudy looks best when he's naked," she said) and his growing celebrity.

The only problem with the couple's May 1922 wedding in Mexicali, Mexico—accompanied by Ivano and Nazimova, a string quartet and a military band they picked up somewhere along the way—was that his divorce from Acker hadn't been finalized. A week later Rudy, as everyone called him, pled guilty to bigamy in a Los Angeles court. Since it was the weekend and the banks were closed, he couldn't raise the $10,000 bail, so the great Rudolph Valentino was thrown in jail like a common criminal. Several hours later bail was met by friends. The bigamy charge was dropped after the couple, along with Ivano and Nazimova, perjured themselves by testifying that the marriage had not been consummated.

That set the scene for a remarriage in Mexico, which, by California law, had to take place no less than a year later, and on the way the couple spent the night at the Palm Springs home of Dr. Florilla White.

It isn't hard to figure out how they all became friends. In 1921 when Valentino had made *The Sheik*, exteriors were said to have been shot near Oxnard, California, and the Guadalupe Dunes area of Santa Barbara, but some of it was filmed near Palm Springs; there are photographs of Valentino in the town at the time. Since Dr. White was the only physician in the area, clearly they met either on the film location or, more likely, at a social event in town.

The question of whether Valentino was gay or bisexual has never gone away; few claim that he was straight. Although the situation is largely forgotten today, Valentino, whom women adored, was loathed by many straight men who made fun of his dress and mannerisms; a *Chicago Tribune* newspaperman referred to men who copied Valentino's romantic style as "pink powder puffs." According to John dos Passos in his docu-novel *The Big Money* from his *U.S.A. Trilogy*, when Valentino came out of anesthesia after his August 1926 operation for a perforated ulcer, he said, "Well, did I behave like a pink powder puff?" Valentino died on August 23, eight days after the operation, when peritonitis set in (fatal in those pre-antibiotics days), an event that plunged the entire world into mourning.

•••••

But, however it happened, the sexually divided Valentino was a friend of Dr. White, close enough to be invited to stay with her on the night before his and Rambova's remarriage. It makes one wonder. But as Valentino himself was aware, how many straight men marry known lesbians?

And how many sexually ambivalent couples would spend the night before a remarriage (imagine the conversation!) with a "straight" mannish physician who just happened to "co-habit" with friends who were very "out" lesbians?

Dr. White died in 1942.

So all one has to go on is the evidence.

# CHAPTER THREE

# LOIS

I f Dr. White hid her possible lesbian activities behind closed doors, a contemporary named Lois Kellogg apparently had no qualms about being as "out," at least in her personal lifestyle, as she would be today.

Like those of White, Kellogg's most famous guests were either openly lesbian (Alla Nazimova was also a friend) or certainly bisexual. When he was in town or working on a film location nearby, Rudolph Valentino would often ride over to Kellogg's house on his black Arabian horse caparisoned with a silver saddle and a silver copy of a Benvenuto Cellini medallion glinting on the headstall of the bridle. Despite claims, the horse he rode around Palm Springs wasn't Jedann, the gray Arabian which, after the actor's death in 1926, would become famous as "the Valentino horse; Jedann was ridden by Valentino only in his last film, *Son of the Sheik*. On arrival at Kellogg's house, Valentino would often cook a Southern Italian meal in her kitchen for himself, Kellogg, and her guests, among who were usually Nazimova and Valentino's wife, Natacha Rambova. Valentino, from Trapani in the Italian boot, was an accomplished chef.

But Kellogg's notoriety as probably the first openly lesbian woman in Palm Springs rests on many other facts as well.

Kellogg apparently arrived from Chicago in the tiny desert community about 1914, when she would have been twenty. In both America and Europe, where she traveled frequently, people remember her as being a singularly beautiful woman with a strong personality, a soft, low voice with which she spoke several languages, and a devastating charm that could captivate everyone she dealt with—maids, salespeople, her friends, and acquaintances.

She was also the niece of an American ambassador to Russia in the early years of the twentieth century (it's intriguing to speculate on whether she would have known Rose Dougan's aristocratic Russian companion, Baroness Vera von Blumenfeld), and was a patron of the arts (she once danced with Chicago's Russian Ballet). Not surprisingly, since she shopped for her clothes more or less exclusively in the Paris salons of Worth, who was then society's top designer, as well as those of Lanvin and Molyneux, she was once voted the best-dressed woman in her hometown.

In 1919 Kellogg bought the land between Palm Canyon Drive and Indian Canyon, where today Staples office supply store stands. It was selected, she claimed, for the view. Kellogg then hired architect Harold Bryant Cody the husband of her close friend Harriet Cody, to design a Persian-Moroccan style palace; the cost-be-damned spread would be the first of the many large estates that soon sprung up in the city. Built of poured concrete with two-foot-thick walls, the huge complex included a vast entrance hall, a thirty-foot ceiling in the drawing room, hand-carved wooden doors, and a "Persian" courtyard reminiscent of a medieval cloister, where vines heavy with gold and red flowers enclosed rows of cypress, fig, and orange trees.

From the house, a tiled Moroccan door led to a 65-foot swimming pool that boasted a pioneering installation of underwater lighting, a dozen varicolored lights that gave it a magical look at night—or so it was said at the time.

Despite her patrician upbringing, Kellogg didn't sit around and watch while the workmen built her home, which she called "my second Babylon," before christening it in the city's lore as "Fool's Folly." In an era when women were largely unaware of how to hammer a nail into a wall, Kellogg joined forces with the construction crew, working daily on the house and loading and running the cement mixer. One day when she was stretched out on the roof hard at work hammering shingles, one of the workmen grabbed her overalled leg—thinking it was one of his fellow workmen—to haul himself onto the roof from a scaffold. Unlike many "proper" women of the day, Kellogg also smoked cigarettes to the shocked disapproval of many. On one occasion, when the train on which she was traveling from Chicago to Palm Springs stopped for breakfast, as was the custom in those days, Kellogg wandered off to smoke a cigarette. When she returned, she found that the train, carrying several of her prized Russian wolfhounds along with her money and baggage, had left. Being a take-charge person, she called a nearby airfield and talked a pilot into flying her to the train's next stop, only to see the train pulling out when she reached that station.

Broke but undaunted, Kellogg proceeded to write checks on scraps of paper to pay the pilot and get a ticket on the next train; her personality was apparently so convincing that these improvised checks were accepted, and she soon linked up with her dogs, money, and luggage. That's the story, anyway.

After Fool's Folly, it was her collection of Russian wolfhounds that made her locally famous. Kellogg supposedly had, at least in later life, up to 200 of the dogs, which were descended from wolfhounds she had bought in Russia before World War I; according

to a contemporary report, she kept 30 at her Palm Springs home
and another 170 at her 3,000-acre stock ranch near Arlemont,
Nevada. In 1934 one of them won the prestigious Palm Springs
dog show at the Desert Inn resort, an event about which it was
reported, "Southern California's society turned out en mass to
see the 400 dogs in the desert show." It also has been speculated
that, after World War I and the Russian Revolution, the breed
was in danger of extinction had Kellogg (accompanied by Harriet Cody) not traveled to Europe, where she gave a breeder in
Belgium one of the descendants of the original pack.

Kellogg clearly was stronger, was more fearless, and pos-
sessed far more energy than people suspected. More important
was her belief that a woman could do anything a man could, and
she proved it over and over again. She, again unlike most women
of her time, had a genius for mechanics, and on one telling occasion, she stunned a local auto mechanic by using a hairpin to re-
pair her rare, worth-its-weight-in-gold, Hispano-Suiza automo-
bile that had developed engine trouble. It is also interesting that
many of the "workmen" she hired to help build Fool's Folly were
women as energetic and unconventional as she was; among them
was one Betty Kapalonoff, who was then introduced as her assistant but was probably, as many today believe, also her lover.

She also had a reputation for being far stronger than she appeared. This fact became clear on one occasion when she, Dr.
White, Palm Springs pioneer Zadie Bunker, Harriet Cody, and
several cowboys were driving Kellogg's herd of pure white,
prize-winning short-horn bulls, which she had imported from
Chicago, up to Bunker's mountain ranch to escape the summer
heat. Along the way Lois saw and fell in love with a little wild
Indian stallion, all black with a white star in the center of his
forehead. The mustang, apparently furious over their presence,
galloped around the women, biting and yanking at the tails of
their horses. Lois somehow maneuvered the horse into a box

canyon and, after three of the men riding with them had given up, Kellogg lassoed the pony. After he twice turned head over heels trying to get away, she also calmed him down and tied him to a tree; the horse would be her favorite for years.

On another occasion she was seen riding one of her bulls from the pasture to the barn. The bull, which had the reputation of having killed three men, was as tame as Bossy in Kellogg's hands.

•••••

Harold Cody died in 1924 and, despite her contacting Frank Lloyd Wright's son, Lloyd (who the previous year had designed the Oasis Hotel in Palm Springs; all that remains of the hotel, which was built around pioneer John McCallum's original adobe house, is the tower at 121 South Palm Canyon Drive), and asking him to finish the house, work on Fool's Folly essentially stopped. Kellogg apparently lived in the unfinished "Babylonian palace" off and on for at least another decade, commuting back and forth to her Nevada ranch. Eventually the growth of Palm Springs began blocking the unobstructed views that had first attracted her to the site, finally convincing her to sell the place,.

After Kellogg left, her mansion stood abandoned, a home for the homeless and the pigeons that roosted in the eves of the cathedral ceilings. In 1939 Kellogg sold the property to the owner of the famous Chi-Chi club and later of the Riviera Hotel. Before the building was torn down and replaced by a Safeway store and now Staples, a few of the finished rooms were used for a short time as classrooms by the local Jewish temple.

Kellogg's end was equally sad. In 1944 she contracted tularemia, a serious, infectious disease (also known as "rabbit fever"), either from cutting up an infected rabbit and puncturing her hand on a contaminated bone or, more likely, by being bitten by one of her beloved wolfhounds. In any event she died twenty days later on August 27

Lois Kellogg's body was taken to Sacramento for cremation and her ashes were spread on the Nevada ranch. She was forty-nine.

# CHAPTER FOUR

## CARY AND RANDY

In 1954 Cary Grant and his third wife, Betsy Drake, bought the sprawling, six-bedroom estate known as Las Palomas (the doves) in the Movie Colony neighborhood of Palm Springs.

Built in 1927, and following the pattern of residential exoticism begun by Lois Kellogg, who started building her never-to-be-finished *Fool's Folly* six years earlier, the place was claimed to be inspired by a nineteenth-century Andalusian farmhouse. Like Grant's five marriages, however, the result was less successful than would be traditionally expected. The handmade clay roof tiles were authentic-looking but, with its (then) blue shutters and architectural allowance for the house's most un-Andalusian cathedral ceilings, the façade at least ended up looking like a displaced Tyrolean barn. Appropriately though, the one-and-a-half-acre site on which it was built was filled with olive and citrus trees, date palms, and rosebushes.

What was Grant's place in Hollywood's hierarchy when he bought the property? He had just turned fifty and had twice been nominated for an Oscar: 1941's *Penny Serenade* and 1944's *None*

*But the Lonely Heart.* (The only Oscar he ever actually received was an honorary one, awarded in 1970). Although such blockbusters as *North by Northwest* and *To Catch a Thief* (the first film he made after moving into the Palm Springs estate) lay in the future, many of his sixty films up that point had already made him immensely popular. Among them were 1933's *She Done Him Wrong*, in which he co-starred with Mae West (he was on the receiving end of West's famous "Why don't you come up and see me sometime?" line); the tremendously popular *Topper* (1937); *Arsenic and Old Lace* (1944); *Notorious* (1946; his second film directed by Alfred Hitchcock, who famously disliked actors but would later claim that Grant was "the only actor I ever loved in my whole life"); and *The Bachelor and the Bobby Soxer* (1947).

Grant was also the first actor to buck the traditional studio system by going independent, gambling that his popularity would allow him, instead of a studio, to control his career, including the movies he would appear in, his directors and co-stars, and even how much he would be paid. Unheard of at the time, the practice is now common.

Grant and Drake would divorce in 1962—during the marriage she famously introduced him to LSD—and he continued to reside, at least part-time, at the house during and after his stormy 1965 to 1968 marriage to Dyan Cannon. Grant lived at the house until 1972, nine years before he would marry his last wife, Barbara Harris. She was forty-seven years younger than the actor and was with him when he died of a cerebral hemorrhage while preparing for a theater performance in Davenport, Iowa, in November 1986. The common wisdom of the time was that, until he moved away from Palm Springs, he lived alone.

Maybe yes, maybe no.

•••••

From his early days in Hollywood, Cary Grant's sexual orientation was as much a subject of conversation as was his fame—at least in Hollywood. Although he would later dance around the subject, and occasionally claim he wasn't gay, in the beginning he did nothing to deny the gossip. The speculation was first fueled by the fact that Grant, before coming to Hollywood in 1931 and still known by his name of Archibald Leach, had shared a tiny walk-up apartment in New York with the gay John Orry-Kelly (who would become famous as one of Hollywood's most prolific costume designers) and an actor named Charles Spangles. Then the rumors moved into high gear when, in 1932, twenty-eight-year-old Grant met another young actor, Randolph Scott, on the set of a Paramount film named *Hot Saturday*. (Grant's screen name came soon after he signed a contract with the studio.)

Something clearly clicked between the pair, since they soon set up housekeeping together in a small apartment and then in a delightful, 5,000-square-foot Spanish Revival house on West Live Oak Drive near Griffith Park in Hollywood.

•••••

To many of their contemporaries in the film capital, there was little doubt that Grant and Scott were lovers, and Grant's "gayness" was openly discussed. Although both Barbara Harris and Betsy Drake denied that he was gay, Grant once admitted that his first two wives, the actress Virginia Cherrill and heiress Barbara Hutton, had accused him of being a homosexual.

Grant's homosexuality also was supported by direct testimony from such friends as director George Cukor; George Burns; the actor's later secretary, Frank Horn; and the gay photographer Jerome Zerbe, who, according to author William Mann, spent three months in Hollywood photographing the pair. He later claimed that they "were very involved in the gay scene." Jimmy Fiedler, a powerful radio gossip columnist of the time, once sniped of Grant's very public friendship with actor Randolph Scott: "These guys are carrying the buddy business a bit too far," and actress Carole Lombard was quoted in the *Los Angeles Times* as saying: "I wonder which of those guys pays the bills." In 1980 Chevy Chase referred to Grant on Tom Snyder's *Tomorrow* show as a "homo." Grant sued and the case was settled out of court. Perhaps the last word on the subject, and clearly an admission of sorts, was uttered by Grant himself in later life: "I pretended to be somebody I wanted to be," he said, "and finally I became that person."

•••••

The studios, terrified by the potential effect that the rapidly shifting morals standards of the 1930s might have on the box office, quickly began pressuring their single male stars to marry. Grant obeyed; two years after moving into the house with Scott, he married Virginia Cherrill, the actress who unforgettably played the blind flower girl opposite Charlie Chaplin in 1931's *City Lights*; she and Grant met at the premiere of *Blonde Venus*, the 1932 film in which he co-starred with Marlene Dietrich. After a "whirlwind romance" (fan magazine terminology for a "short engagement"), they married on February 10, 1934, in England. When they returned, standing at the doorstep to welcome the newlyweds as Grant carried Cherrill over the threshold of their Hollywood home, was Randolph Scott (as well as Grant's dog, named Archie Leach).

Not surprisingly, it wasn't long before all this togetherness became too much. Within months the newlyweds moved to the La Ronda Apartments in Hollywood, reportedly because Cherrill couldn't put up with Scott being around all the time. Scott, responding to similar studio pressure, married heiress Marian duPont Somerville in 1936, whereupon he followed Grant—who had separated from Cherrill in 1935—to the La Ronda, where they lived in adjoining apartments.

Early in his relationship with Cherrill, Grant apparently became so unhappy that he began drinking heavily, became surly in private, and attempted suicide at least once. Nevertheless after his 1935 divorce from Virginia Cherrill (she charged him with hitting her), Grant was reported in the Hollywood press to be having an impassioned affair with the starlet Betty Furness, later of Westinghouse commercials fame, and also with Mary Brian, his co-star in 1936's *The Amazing Adventure*. During the next two years the fan magazines started to refer to Phyllis Brooks, a leading lady in Hollywood "B" pictures from the mid-1930s to mid-1940s, as the "next Mrs. Grant." "I'm going to marry Brooksie," the fan magazines quoted him as saying, "and have all the children we can. That's what life is all about." Within two months, in the fall of 1939, the pair became engaged and then broke up.

Norma Talmadge was one of the greatest of the silent film stars considered by many later commentators as possessing a talent and a beauty that no later arrival—whether a Marlene Dietrich or a Greta Garbo—could ever replace. She enjoyed a career that reached back to the very beginnings of the industry. For F. Scott Fitzgerald she was the epitome of 1920s glamour; in his 1934 novel *Tender Is the Night* he recalled her jazz-age image as reflecting someone who "must be a fine, noble woman beyond her loveliness. Unfortunately for Talmadge, as for many others at the time, the luster of fame tarnished quickly after the arrival of sound in 1928. Nevertheless, in 1929 she built a (still-standing) Santa Monica beach house in a style that could be dismissed as "Hollywood Tudor" had it not cost so much—

$550,000 plus $120,000 for the beach property, the equivalent of some $30 $40 million for beach property today. Her career was over, as was her marriage to Joseph Schenck, the first president of United Artists (who had personally guided her film career and was by then chairman of Twentieth Century Fox).

In 1939 Talmadge remarried and sold her house to Cary Grant, who lived there with Randolph Scott. There is a story that Grant and Scott loved the place so much that they agreed that whichever of them remarried first would have the option to own it. But things didn't quite work out that way. After several years of dating and breaking up with a number of women—but never with Scott—within a month after becoming an American citizen on June 26, 1942, Grant married the Woolworth heiress Barbara Hutton. But Scott stayed. Hutton once recalled of the *ménage à trois*: "Come to think of it, that fellow never did move out. He was always in a back room somewhere." Hutton usually had nice things to say about Cary, once telling dinner guests that Grant was the only man in her life who had never wanted anything from her. "Not even sex," murmured one guest.

None of this would stop Grant from installing a luxurious dressing room for himself in the beach house (apparently Scott lived somewhere in the attic); nor did it stop Hutton from trying to turn the place into a sort of Paris-west. As World War II was raging at the time, she declared: "If I can't go to Paris, Paris must come to me." To her, that meant redesigning a bar in the sunroom, adding carved woodwork in the downstairs powder room, and transforming the dining room into a space reminiscent of Maxim's, her favorite Paris restaurant. Deep ruby-red plush banquettes seating twenty-four at silver-colored tables were installed around the room, and the slate floor was covered with matching red carpet. On the walls, gold-flecked, smoked-glass mirrors were installed.

Grant also decided to fill the pool with fresh water rather than sea water, as was the custom at beach houses of the time. "After all," he remarked, "if I want to bathe in sea water, all I have to do is open the gate, go down the steps and walk in." He also added a filter but somehow neglected a heater.

Paradise? Well, for a time it seemed to be. But by 1945 the marriage—the couple were derisively referred to in the popular press as "Cash and Cary"—was on its last legs. Hutton was always difficult and also had expectations of the marriage that were different from Grant's; he attributed this problem to the public's tendency to mistake a film star's screen persona with his or her real self. "She thought she was marrying Cary Grant," he said. Hutton offered Grant a money settlement in the divorce, which he refused, and they remained friends for years.

Not long before their divorce, Grant and Hutton moved into a larger place, clearing the way for Scott, who had divorced his previous wife and married actress Patricia Stillman, to take over the beach house in 1944. In 1946 Scott sold the house to British actor Brian Aherne and his new wife, who occasionally rented out the place, most famously to Howard Hughes—who topped the walls with barbed wire (some of which still remains)—and to Roman Polanski and his wife Sharon Tate. Tate, in fact, was living at the house when she was killed in the Charles Manson massacre in August 1969—Polanski was in Europe. The Scotts would adopt two children and remain married for forty-three years until the actor's death in 1987.

Aherne claimed that Grant always regretted selling the beach house to Scott and often asked the British actor in later years, "Oh, sell it back to me." Aherne claims Grant also sometimes added: "Come to think of it, I don't think Randy ever paid me for the place."

In 1947 Merle Oberon introduced Cary Grant to Betsy Drake, an American actress returning from an engagement in

London, on board the luxury liner *Queen Mary*. They quickly became friends and were romantically involved. It wasn't a hard call for Grant, then one of the biggest male stars in Hollywood, to convince RKO to sign Drake to the then standard seven-year contract and cast her in his next film project, the romantic comedy *Every Girl Should Be Married*. According to Charles Higham and Roy Moseley, authors of *Cary Grant: The Lonely Heart*, Grant, who by then had become extremely manipulative, watched every move Betsy made on the set and involved himself in every aspect of her performance, from dialogue to lighting to hairstyles and costumes.

Released with fanfare as RKO's big 1948 Christmas picture, the film was a financial success. The couple married exactly one year later, and the union would last for thirteen years—the longest of his five marriages.

Grant first saw Dyan Cannon on the short-lived television adventure *Malibu Run* in 1961. After a lengthy (for Grant) courtship, they eloped on July 22, 1965; Grant was 61, Cannon 26. Six months later their daughter, Jennifer, was born; nevertheless the marriage was troubled from the beginning and the couple separated after a year and a half, in December 1966. Cannon claimed that Grant flew into frequent rages and spanked her when she "disobeyed" him. She later elaborated about her "Pygmalion relationship" with Grant, and, indeed as with Drake, his opinions on her clothes, makeup, and career choices were law. Their divorce, finalized in March 1968, was bitter and messy, and the custody disputes over their daughter raged on for another decade. Eventually they reestablished their friendship, but Grant was bitter about Cannon's behavior for years.

Cary Grant and Barbara Harris, a British public relations agent, first met in 1976, four years after he sold the Palm Springs estate and moved back into Beverly Hills. It was there that they married on April 15, 1981, with only his daughter, Jennifer, his lawyer, Stanley Fox, and his wife; and a judge and his wife present. "Grant's last marriage was a quiet and happy one. He had finally found a relationship that worked," was the coda of a recent short biography of the actor. Or was he just too old to worry?

•••••

Recently a photograph dating from the mid-1950s surfaced in Palm Springs showing Grant and Drake riding at the city's Shadow Mountain resort. Another photograph has also turned up from the same period showing Randolph Scott—alone—riding at the same stable. At the time, Scott also rented or owned a home in Indian Wells, a resort community adjoining Palm Springs.

In an earlier book I mentioned that the relationship between Grant and Scott endured for eleven years during their separate marriages—more or less until the Santa Monica beach house was sold. On the basis of the Palm Springs evidence, it seems that the relationship—certainly the friendship—probably lasted far longer. Despite being married to Stillman, Scott was clearly spending time in the desert not far from his one-time lover more than twenty years after they first met.

Earlier I quoted Grant as saying of his career (and perhaps his lifestyle): "I pretended to be somebody I wanted to be," he said, "and finally I became that person." Given the persistence of Scott's presence as well as the emotional conflicts that assaulted Grant throughout his life, perhaps he was fibbing when he said that he finally "became the person he wanted to be." Maybe he was that person all along, the loving soul mate of Randolph Scott throughout a lifetime that was, certainly in part, a pretense dictated by his career.

In any event, at least some of the final chapters in the pair's lifelong relationship were played out in Palm Springs.

# CHAPTER FIVE

# GINNY AND LANA AND
# JOHNNY AND CHERYL

As it has proven to be for many full-time residents, Palm Springs began as a weekend getaway spot for city council member Ginny Foat, a lesbian, when she bought a home in the desert in 1992 after being drawn there by the Dinah Shore weekend. ("I didn't come for the golf, I came for the party," she laughs. "Now I also go for the golf.")

Foat may have come for the party, but what really transformed her life was a defining attribute of the community: its atmosphere of tolerance; of people "accepting the other's talents," she says. "I can't remember when I last went to an all-gay party here," Foat added, rushing to a city council meeting. "You go to parties now and it's always straight and gay together, both accepting the other's talents. I also can't remember any issues that have come before the city council that pitted gays and straights against each other. My challenges with my partner of twenty years are the same challenges anyone has, like 'How do you find a good gardener?'"

And no one's life better epitomizes the transformational na-ture of tolerance than Ginny's own. Today she walks the streets of Palm Springs recognized as a city council member and (at the writing), as mayor pro-tem of the city who just happens to be a lesbian in a longtime committed relationship with her partner, Pamela Genevrino.

But twenty-five years ago she was—thanks to a vicious media feeding frenzy fueled in part by the right-wing, antiabortionist, anti-feminist movement—notorious as a twice-accused murderer. Foat's abusive husband, Jack Sidote, had implicated her in the murder of a hotel executive in Nevada. When the crime came to trial in 1977, Sidote refused to testify against Foat, and she was released for lack of evidence.

Then in January 1983, two years after Foat was elected as the first paid president of the California chapter of the National Organization of Women (NOW), the four-time-married feminist was arrested for the brutal bludgeoning murder seventeen years earlier of an Argentine businessman in New Orleans. This time, in a deal Sidote made with the local district attorney to avoid being tried for this murder, he implicated Foat again.

She was found "not guilty" on November 16, 1983, after a trial that was publicized around the world (the jury deliberated for only forty-five minutes during which they also took a lunch break). Within hours of the verdict, she broke her silence on the case, telling reporters that the verdict was "a victory for all women whose plight in life is to have to stay in a position because of social mores."

But it was exactly those social mores—or more accurately, the era's conflict between new and traditional social mores—that made the case an international cause célèbre. And the controversy didn't end with the verdict: Was her acquittal a victory for a noble cause, as she and her feminist supporters proclaimed? Or was it a miscarriage of justice for a femme fatale, as some right-wing Web sites still proclaim?

In her 1985 autobiography *Never Guilty, Never Free*, Foat tells the story of a girl who was born to an Italian family and raised in working-class neighborhoods in Brooklyn and Queens, New York. She was always a tomboy, who once set a vacant lot on fire with a carelessly discarded match or cigarette butt. Nevertheless her toughness didn't protect her from painful whippings by her father, who kept a leather strap for that purpose hanging in their basement.

Foat, who in later years would be physically, emotionally, and legally abused by a husband who had no compunction about implicating her in a murder to save his skin, would become a spokesperson for abused women. But in her book she also asked herself a serious question: "I've wondered whether it might have been there, in that basement, that I first began to believe in the rightness, the acceptability, of being beaten by a man I loved."

Not surprisingly, when she first ran for Palm Springs' city council in 2003, the lurid story of twenty years past was dredged up by the local newspaper, the *Desert Sun*, in a fashion that can only be described as exploitive. "For 11 months in 1983," Brian Joseph wrote in the community's journal of record, "she was a celebrity of the worst kind, a figure of similar prominence to Sam Sheppard or O. J. Simpson or Kobe Bryant—her every turn a front page story, her every word a quote."

Fighting back, she wrote a lengthy piece available on the Internet (at *www.2000colors.com/voteto2t/real.htm*), while also revealing that her husband tried to kill her:

"Through their own brand of slanted journalism, the *Desert Sun* has chosen to write about my past rather than the future of this city.

"Somewhere around 1965 in the height of the Vietnam war protests, the peace-child and hippy era and the time when many young people were traveling the country, I met and married a man that turned out to be a monster.

"My life took on the tumultuousness of the times I was battered and abused by this man until my escape from him in the early 70's. After a failed attempt on my life and his murder of another human being he was sent to prison and I thought I was finally free.

"In 1979 I answered a knock on my door and the nightmare of this monster began again. In an effort to get a reduction in his prison sentence he accused me of two horrendous crimes of which I had no knowledge or complicity. He offered his testimony in exchange for that reduction. I was arrested and incarcerated awaiting extradition to Nevada where he claimed one of the crimes had taken place. I was extradited and held for a short period of time until the evidence was brought before a judge and thrown out of court.

"In 1983 the nightmare began again. I was arrested and spent another couple of months incarcerated awaiting extradition to New Orleans where he claimed I had committed another murder again seeking a reduction in his sentence. This time I was not alone. People from throughout the country mobilized around my defense. My huge bail was posted by a New Orleans doctor and monies for my defense came from all over the country. I went to trial where he, on the guarantee of immunity and a recommendation for a reduced sentence, testified against me. It quickly became apparent to all that were involved that he had created this accusation for his own personal gain. The jury deliberated for 45 minutes during which time they ate lunch and came back with a not guilty verdict."

As the *Desert Sun* pointed out in their 2003 piece (while at the same time reminding their readers again of the purported crime):

"Time has a way of making a once-famous face ordinary again." And, in the case of Ginny Foat, her real background, one committed to community service, political leadership, and business development, including a decade as executive director of Los Angeles' Caring for Babies with AIDS organization, is what defines her today—at least in Palm Springs.

"Today her passions are as strong as ever, but they are directed toward the community's well-being and growth. 'There were a lot of bad decisions in the past,' she says of the city's development, 'a totally business-unfriendly atmosphere and a lot else. Then gays and lesbians moved in and took over entire neighborhoods and became absolutely enthralled with the mid-century modern architecture that we have here—it was cheap as dirt then—and rejuvenated many parts of town.'

"'Much has changed for the better,' she says of the Palm Springs' open and tolerant nature since she joined the city council in 2003. She claims that she has never felt ill at ease about being a lesbian. 'I never felt uncomfortable going to a restaurant or holding hands with my girlfriend in public from the time we moved here,' she says.

"'But recently, the more they saw our communities, I think the city has become far more understanding of the issues affecting gays and lesbians. As one example, the police department has become much more aware of hate crimes. And in my first year on the council, I introduced a resolution condemning George Bush for his support of a constitutional amendment banning gay marriage—which passed four to zero with one member of our council absent. And we just signed an amicus brief with the California State Supreme Court supporting what happened in San Francisco supporting marriage, and that was a 4-1 vote. We have now elected a (gay) mayor who, with his partner, has two children.'

"The old guard is on their way out."

•••••

Many current biographies of Cheryl Crane, a permanent resident of Palm Springs since March 1996, claim that she came out as a lesbian when she was in her thirties. Crane, however, told the author that she was only twelve when she informed her famous mother, Lana Turner, that "I was in love with a woman." She also claims that she and her partner, Jocelyn "Josh" LeRoy, met when they were in kindergarten. "Josh and I have always been 'out' in a mixed society," Crane says today, "and she [Lana] loved and adored Josh, whom she considered a second daughter—we were a family." Crane adds that she and her mother would often visit Palm Springs when she was a child, sometimes staying at a resort or sometimes she would rent a house; it was the place everyone went to despite the fact that there was no freeway then. Today both Crane and LeRoy are successful realtors in the resort town.

"One of the most interesting things about Palm Springs today," Crane adds, "is that there is really no longer a gay ghetto. It used to be that gays went only to gay bars. But there is none of that kind of segregation anymore."

When she was fourteen, Crane was arrested for the murder of Johnny Stompanato, her mom's boyfriend, a hoodlum with ties to mobster Mickey Cohen—and there is no question that she was guilty.

And the press hoopla over the Good Friday 1958 killing makes the media craze over Ginny Foat's trials seem laughably tame.

First a little about Lana Turner for those too young to remember her name and stunning blonde beauty. Dubbed "the sweater girl" at sixteen for the form-fitting outfit she wore in her first film, 1937's *They Won't Forget*, Turner would define Hollywood glamour for more than a generation during which she made sixty films. In 1956, when she was thirty-five, Turner and her fourth husband, Lex Barker (a famous film Tarzan), came to the desert and rented a weekend house in nearby Palm Desert, long before that community, now famed for its shopping and elegant restaurants, boasted little more than a filling station and a small restaurant.

It has been said that Hollywood lives on its own legends. And no legend is more famous than the one about Turner's "discovery" at the then-popular Schwab's Drugstore in Hollywood. It isn't true, but the facts are close enough. Turner, then a student at Hollywood High and known as Judy Turner, decided one day in 1937 to cut a typing class and buy a Coke at the long-gone Top Hat Café directly across the street from the famous high school.

While perched at the counter, Turner was spotted by William Wilkerson, publisher of *The Hollywood Reporter*, and his wife, Tichi. Said to have been impressed with her adolescent beauty (as well as, certainly, of her natural, uh, endowments), Wilkerson arranged for her to meet Zeppo Marx, who in addition to being one of the famous Marx Brothers film comedy team, was also a talent agent. Marx's agency signed her and arranged a film test with director Mervyn LeRoy, who cast her—still sixteen—in *They Won't Forget*. Later that year she had a bit part in the original *A Star Is Born* starring Fredric March and Janet Gaynor. (Henry Willson, who later became notorious for running a "beefcake" agency and inventing names for his stars, including Tab Hunter, was then an employee of Marx and is said to have been responsible for changing her name to "Lana.")

Because of the huge success of her early films—among them *Ziegfield Girl* (1941), *Johnny Eager* (1942), and the first two of four films co-starring with MGM's biggest male star, Clark Gable (*Honky Tonk* in 1940, and *Somewhere I'll Find You* in 1942)—as well as her breathtaking physique, she became a tremendously popular pinup girl during World War II, probably second only in popularity to the leggy Betty Grable.

After the war her career reached its zenith when she co-starred with John Garfield in the early film noir classic *The Postman Always Rings Twice*. Despite an erosion of popularity in the 1950s, Turner was widely praised for her performance in Vincente Minnelli's *The Bad and the Beautiful* (1952) and received a Best Actress Oscar nomination for her performance in the screen adaptation of Grace Metalious's best-selling novel *Peyton Place*. Then, probably because of the notoriety over Stompanato's murder, Ross Hunter's remake of the 1934 film *Imitation of Life* starring Claudette Colbert (Chapter 6), became one of the biggest hits of 1959 and the greatest success of Turner's career. Oddly, both *Peyton Place* and *Imitation of Life* dealt with a single mother coping with a troubled teenage daughter—another example of how Hollywood exploited the challenges and tragedies of its own stars if doing so meant good box office.

Turner was married eight times to seven men, among them bandleader Artie Shaw, whom she stayed with for only four months (married to him at nineteen, Turner referred to the experience as her "college education"); millionaire Henry Topping Jr. (the gossip columnists of the time made much over his proposing by dropping a diamond engagement ring into her martini at Manhattan's 21 Club); twice to Cheryl's father, an actor-restaurateur named Stephen Crane (the first marriage was annulled after it was discovered that his previous divorce hadn't been finalized; they remarried after a brief separation during which Crane attempted suicide); and Lex Barker (whom Turner divorced in 1957 after the thirteen-year-old Cheryl confided to her mom that he had raped her).

Turner replaced Barker with a two-bit mobster named Johnny

Stompanato, who had two nicknames that pretty well defined his credentials: "Handsome Harry" for his reputation for romancing older women and then taking their money, and "Oscar" because, reportedly, his penis was supposedly the size of the Academy Award statuette. He also had a reputation for abusing women and, in fact, attempted to strangle Turner when she refused to make him executive producer of her film *Another Time, Another Place*, made in early 1958 in England. Reportedly, Stompanato also pointed a gun at Turner's co-star, Sean Connery, who, as at least one observer says, "did a pre-James Bond turn by grabbing the gun out of Stompanato's hand, beating him with it, and leveling the Lothario in lizard shoes."

On March 24, 1958, Turner appeared on the live Oscar television broadcast as a Best Actress nominee for her role in *Peyton Place*, the second highest–grossing film of 1957. She lost to Joanne Woodward's performance in *The Three Faces of Eve*. On her return home, Stompanato, furious that she had taken Cheryl with her to the Academy Awards instead of him, brutally beat her. Turner would later reflect on "the bitter irony of a battered woman in diamonds struck me like another blow from John's fist." Several days later she confided to Cheryl Crane that she feared for her safety but wouldn't go to the police because "no one must know."

Then eleven days later, on Good Friday, April 4, three days after Turner, Crane, and Johnny moved into Lana's new house in Beverly Hills, the couple fought again. Turner, then thirty-seven, seemingly had discovered that Stompanato was thirty-three-years-old, not forty-three, as he had told her, and she was furious. "He's making me feel like one of those old has-beens you see around who pay for young men," she reportedly told her daughter.

When Stompanato returned to the house later that night, Turner told him it was all over, and he threatened to kill her.

Crane, who was doing her homework in her room, was terrified by the noise, ran down to the kitchen, grabbed a 10-inch butcher knife they had bought that afternoon for the new kitchen (she took it in order to scare him, she later claimed), ran to her mother's room, and banged on the door. Reportedly she heard Stompanato say, "You'll never get away from me. I'll cut you good, baby. No one will ever look at that pretty face again." The gangster then ran out of the room and "ran onto the knife," Crane later testified. It punctured his kidney and aorta and he died on the carpet. His last words before he collapsed were reported to be: "My God, Cheryl, what have you done?" before he collapsed.

The distraught Turner's first words to the Beverly Hills police chief (who was irked to see that Jerry Geisler, the "attorney to the stars," had arrived before he did) were, "Can I take the blame for this horrible thing?" "No, not unless you have committed the act, Miss Turner," said the chief. Eventually she mumbled, "Okay, it was my daughter."

Cheryl was taken to the police station. The next day Los Angeles County district attorney William B. McKesson said he was dissatisfied with Turner's version of events and announced a coroner's inquest for the following week to determine if Cheryl Crane should be charged with murder, which, despite her age, carried a life sentence if she was found guilty.

The coroner's inquest, however, ruled that the death was justifiable homicide (observers said Turner's testimony was the best acting of her life). Nevertheless, McKesson, convinced that Cheryl had never had a real life with her mother or father, had her declared a ward of the state after she spent three weeks in Juvenile Hall. She was sent to a home for problem girls, from which she escaped in 1960; she was recaptured, and then released in 1961.

Fast-forward a generation. On March 6, 1995, Lana, weighing only eighty-five pounds, was admitted to Cedars Sinai Medical Center because her jaw and neck were severely swollen from throat cancer. One reporter claimed that the doctors wanted to remove Lana's jawbone but that the actress refused—"My face was my fortune," she said, "and I want to be able to look in a mirror right up until the end. I'm going to go out like a star." Released, in apparently good spirits despite the prospect of weeks of radiation therapy, she went home.

Lana Turner died on Thursday, June 29, 1995, her daughter at her side. She was seventy-four years old. She left $50,000 and her fur coats to Cheryl and the balance of her large estate to her maid/companion of forty years, Carmen Lopez Cruz.

# CHAPTER SIX

# KATE AND CLAUDETTE
# AND GRETA AND...

lthough rarely discussed at the time because of box office concerns—nothing is sacred in Hollywood except protecting the movie box office—it was common knowledge within the industry during Hollywood's so-called golden age that such stars as Greta Garbo, Marlene Dietrich, Talullah Bankhead, Janet Gaynor, and Barbara Stanwyck were part of a huge underground lesbian, or at least bisexual, element in Hollywood society.

Until the 1930s when the film capital began censoring itself and forcing under cover many sexually ambivalent men such as Cary Grant and Randolph Scott—and later in the 1950s when witch hunts like those led by Senator Joseph McCarthy and the (U.S.) House Un-American Activities Committee did the same for others—Hollywood's lesbian population was, like the film capital's huge gay population, an open secret. It was acknowledged and dealt with by the industry, as with any other power base or trade union, but not in the media, which made references to homosexuality in the all-too-coy jargon of the time. Garbo's current inamorata would be called her "gal pal," and the actress herself was referred to as the "ambidextrous foreign star" or "the most talked about woman in Hollywood is the woman no wife fears."

Among them was Claudette Colbert, one of the brightest shining stars of Hollywood's greatest years, whose life at the height of her celebrity was intertwined with Palm Springs, where in the late 1950s she even owned a jewelry shop.

On July 30,1996, Colbert died at the age of ninety-two at her ocean-front home, Belle-rive, in Speightstown, Barbados. By then she had long outlived both of her husbands, the first one an actor named Norman Foster, who appeared with her in her 1930's *Young Man of Manhattan* (Ginger Rogers, who one day would spend winters—and die—in nearby Rancho Mirage, also co-starred). Her second husband, Dr. Joel Pressman, a surgeon whom she married four months after her divorce in 1935, died in 1968. Her brother, Charles, who as her agent and business manager, got her many of her most lucrative film deals in the 1930s and 1940s, died in 1971.

She had no children, and the bulk of her $3.5 million estate, including the house in Barbados and a Manhattan apartment, was left to a friend, Helen O'Hagan, a retired director of corporate relations at Saks Fifth Avenue, whom Colbert had met in 1961 on the set of her last film, 1961's *Parrish* (she played the mother of Troy Donahue's character), and who cared for Colbert after a series of strokes in 1993.

Such was the common wisdom of the time.

What is little remembered today is that this woman, who for a generation was one of the most famous actresses in the world, not only lived at least part-time in Palm Springs, but also owned an exclusive jewelry store on Palm Canyon Drive, where, in the late 1950s, she would often personally wait on her customers. In 1960 Colbert sold the shop—located in what is now the Agua Caliente Cultural Museum at the Village Green (221 South Palm

Canyon Drive)—to Jolie Gabor (Zsa-Zsa's mom), who would specialize there in costume jewelry and cultured pearls.

What is probably more accepted today is that Colbert, despite her two marriages and her conservative politics, was a lesbian. It all started, or at least first became public, in 1946 when she shacked up for a time with Katherine Hepburn in a Palm Springs house that Hepburn rented for $500 a month. The story was revealed by their houseboy, Paul Krueger, then twenty-four, who was apparently somewhat famous for "servicing" women visitors (but also claimed he had gone to bed with Charles Farrell, the co-founder of the Racquet Club and mayor of Palm Springs from 1953 to 1960; see Chapter 10). After Krueger reportedly was paid $5,000 in 1955 by *Confidential* magazine, he revealed that when Hepburn and Colbert occupied the house, they "weren't a bit interested in him but went for each other." The story, like *Confidential*'s planned exposé of Rock Hudson at the same time, eventually was buried in the magazine's morgue after Hepburn was said to have paid the magazine $25,000.

There were rumors at the time that Colbert was a lesbian, probably generated from her known association with many women friends and the fact that both of her marriages were, to say the least, unique. She and her first husband, film actor/director Norman Foster, lived apart, never sharing a home together in Hollywood. Instead Colbert chose to live with her widowed mother, Jeanne (her father died in 1925), by then a domineering influence on Colbert. When Foster's film, *Young Man of Manhattan*, was released, it was obvious, at least to one film critic, that their relationship was anything but normal; after noting that Foster was among the weakest of her leading men up to that time, the reviewer added: "He [Foster] did not seem to get any sincerity into his love scenes."

And, despite the length of her thirty-three-year marriage to Dr. Pressman, his main duty in the relationship seems to have been to be her companion at industry and social events. In fact, when Colbert moved back to New York City in the 1950s—and spending some of her time in Palm Springs, at least during 1958 and 1959 when she owned the jewelry shop—she and her husband lived essentially apart, with Dr. Pressman continuing on as a surgeon at UCLA.

· · · · ·

She was born Lily Claudette Chauchoin on September 13, 1903, in Paris, to Georges Claude Chauchoin, a banker and diplomat, and his wife, Jeanne. The family emigrated to the United States when Claudette was three years old and settled in New York City in 1906, where Claudette became a naturalized citizen, attended public schools, and eventually worked as a stenographer and a women's clothing salesclerk.

A small role on Broadway in 1923's *The Wild Westcotts*, written by a friend, Anne Morrison, convinced her that her calling was a stage career—rather than a career as a fashion designer. She soon added Colbert—her paternal grandmother's maiden name—to Claudette, her middle name, which she had used earlier in several high school plays. After critical acclaim in the Broadway production of *The Banker*, she was offered a role in the lost 1927 film *For the Love of Mike*, her only silent movie (and one of the last, since sound came in the following year). In 1928 Claudette signed a contract with Paramount, and a legendary Hollywood career commenced the next year with *The Hole in the Wall*, co-starring Edward G. Robinson. By the time she played the Roman empress Poppea in Cecil B. DeMille's *The Sign of the Cross* in 1932—in which she notoriously bathed in a marble pool filled, supposedly, with "asses' milk"—Colbert had made seventeen films and co-starred opposite such legends as Fredric March and Maurice Chevalier.

It was, however, a film that she "hated" (until, of course, the film won the Oscar and she won the Best Actress Oscar) that made her an international celebrity. It was, of course, Frank Capra's *It Happened One Night* (1934), in which she co-starred with Clark Gable, as a fast-talking, spoiled socialite named El-lie Andrews (Capra later recalled, "Colbert fretted, pouted and argued about her part.... She was a tartar, but a cute one"). That year she also returned to Rome—at least a Hollywood set pass-ing for Rome—by starring in Cecil B. DeMille's 1934 epic *Cleopatra* (many rate her performance, as campy as it seems today, far more acceptable than that of Elizabeth Taylor's effort opposite Rex Harrison a generation later). After making three films with DeMille in which she was seminude, she refused to do any more, probably because of her innate conservatism.

Within a year after the release of *It Happened One Night*, Colbert was selected by movie exhibitors as one of the top ten mon-eymaking stars in the United States. Three years later she was the highest paid performer in Hollywood, making $426,924, the equivalent of over $6 million today. Although she was consid-ered at her best in comedies—Preston Sturges' classic screwball comedy *The Palm Beach Story* is considered by many to be her best film—Colbert also made several successful dramas in the era, including *Boom Town* (1940, with Clark Gable) and 1946's *Without Reservation*, in which she co-starred with John Wayne. In 1945 she left Paramount Pictures and made seven films with Fred MacMurray over the next thirteen years, among them 1947's *The Egg and I*, which was one of the most profitable films of the decade and placed her in the top ten moneymaking list again. The following year she was replaced by her one-time girl-friend, Katherine Hepburn, in the leading role in *State of the Union* because of Colbert's disagreements with the film's direc-tor, Frank Capra.

By 1950 her film career had started to wind down, but not before she nearly got a role that Bette Davis turned into a career tour de force. When Joseph L. Mankiewicz began working on the screenplay of *All About Eve*, he wrote it with Claudette Colbert in mind for the leading role of Margo Channing, since, according to Mankiewicz, she represented the style of actress with a "sly wit and sense of class" that he envisioned for the part of the "elegant drunk." Colbert, unfortunately, was forced to withdraw from the project just before production was to begin after severely injuring her back making *Three Came Home*. Although production was delayed two months—by Mankiewicz, who also directed the film—in hopes that she would recover sufficiently to make it, Colbert was unable to do so and was replaced in the part by Bette Davis, who would famously utter one of the movie's (and Mankiewicz's) most famous lines: "Hold onto your seats, it's going to be a bumpy night."

Famous for playing shrewd and self-reliant women in most of her sixty-three feature films, Colbert was also what later would be called a workaholic. Irene Dunne, the five-time Academy Award–nominated actress perhaps most famous for co-starring with Cary Grant in 1940's *My Favorite Wife* and 1947's *Life with Father*, once said that she lacked Colbert's "terrifying ambition," adding that if Colbert finished work on a film on a Saturday, she would be looking for a new project by Monday. Gossip columnist Hedda Hopper, who along with her rival Louella Parsons was one of the most powerful women in Hollywood at the time, once wrote that Colbert placed her career ahead of everything "save possibly her marriage" and described her as the "smartest and canniest" of Hollywood actresses, with a strong sense of what was best for her and a "deep-rooted desire to be in shape, efficient and under control."

There is more than a little of what was the film capital's double talk in her use of the word "possibly," since Hopper certainly knew about Colbert's lesbian activities. Hopper was also a friend of the actress, and in fact convinced her to take a role in 1943's *So Proudly We Hail!* Not only did her role in this film convince David O. Selznick that he wanted Colbert for *Since You Went Away*, he also was impressed by her box office clout, remarking that "even light little comedies with her have never done under a million and a half."

There is a famous anecdote associated with Colbert that took place between the female co-stars during the filming of *So Proudly We Hail!* As reported in *Movie Talk* by David Shipman (as well as elsewhere) it seems that Colbert overheard a remark by Paulette Goddard, who had recently split from her long relationship with Charles Chaplin. When Goddard was asked which of her colleagues, Colbert or Veronica Lake, was better to work with, she replied, "Veronica, I think. After all, we are closer in age." According to Lake, Colbert "flipped" and "was at Paulette's eyes at every moment" and for the rest of the filming. Goddard, at thirty-three, was in fact closer to Colbert's age (40), than to Veronica Lake's (24).

Besides winning the Oscar for *It Happened One Night* in 1934, Colbert was also nominated for an Academy Award for Best Actress two years later for *Private Worlds*, and again in 1945 for *Since You Went Away*. She was nominated for Broadway's 1959 Tony Award as Best (Dramatic) Actress for *The Marriage-Go-Round*, and she won the 1980 Sarah Siddons Award for Best Actress to play in Chicago for the season 1979–1980 for her performance in the play, *The Kingfisher*. In 1987, at the age of eighty-four, she returned to television in the two-part film, *The Two Mrs. Grenvilles*, opposite Ann-Margret, and was nominated for an Emmy Award for Outstanding Supporting Actress in a Miniseries or a Special. In 1988 she won the Golden Globe Award for Best Performance by an Actress in a Supporting Role in a Series, Miniseries, or Motion Picture made for TV. In 1989 she was awarded the Kennedy Center Honors.

In his book *Katherine the Great*, Darwin Porter claims Kather ine Hepburn also had a long-time relationship with the American Express heiress Laura Harding as well as affairs with Judy Garland, Judy Holliday, and Irene Selznick, daughter of Louis B. Mayer and wife of David O. Selznick, who produced several of Colbert's most successful films. According to Porter, Hepburn also had affairs with many A-list men of the era including Ernest Hemingway, director John Ford, and actors John Barrymore, Douglas Fairbanks Jr., Robert Mitchum, and Burt Lancaster. He also claims she had an affair with Greta Garbo.

Garbo, who was certainly the most secretive of Hollywood stars (although not about her lesbianism, which she more or less flouted during affairs with poet and writer Mercedes de Acosta and with Marlene Dietrich), is the star in one of Palm Springs' most famous "was she there, or wasn't she" stories of the time.

For some reason, which has never been convincingly explained, when MGM decided to premiere *Camille*, one of Garbo's most celebrated movies, and one considered by many as her best performance, they apparently chose to do so in both New York City and Palm Springs on the same day, December 12, 1936. In the desert resort, the event took place in conjunction with the opening of the Plaza Theater, today famous as the site of the popular Palm Springs Follies, basically a vaudeville show featuring stars of yesteryear living in the desert community. (In 1990 the theater was, appropriately enough, the place chosen to screen *Cinema Paradiso* on the opening night of the first Palm Springs International Film Festival, a project Mayor Sonny Bono came up with to restore the then-faded prestige of the resort town.)

So why did MGM decide on a double-barreled opening, and why in Palm Springs, 120 miles from Tinseltown? No one is still around to explain, but it may well have been because MGM understandably wanted a big-city opening, and Greta Garbo, not only the studio's biggest star but the most famous movie star in the world at the time, wanted it to be in one of her favorite places to "be (more or less) alone," Palm Springs. So they did both.

Newspaper records confirm that she was staying at the Ingleside Inn at the time, and Earle Strebe, the owner of the theater, told a reporter in 1990 that Garbo was snuck in late to a balcony seat at the premiere. "She wore slacks and a little dark hat. I caught a glimpse of her in the audience…it was so exciting"—as it probably was for the other celebrities and guests in the audience who paid $2.75 for a reserved seat (the equivalent of $45 today in a time when the average movie ticket was 25 cents).

Among those celebrities filling the 800-seat theater was Garbo's co-star, Robert Taylor, Barbara Stanwyck (who, although linked to many known lesbians, wed Taylor in 1939 in a studio-arranged union), Tyrone Power, Ralph Bellamy, the film's famous (and famously gay) director George Cukor, the popular singer Rudy Vallee, and Hearst gossip columnist Louella Parsons, who hosted a live radio broadcast of the evening's festivities. Supposedly, buried somewhere within the walls of the theater is a time capsule containing the actual print of *Camille* that was shown there at the premiere.

Explaining why the site may have been chosen for the premiere is certainly in line with Garbo's well-known passion for privacy. Clarence May, the projectionist of the night (and for the next fifty years) has said: "The reason the movie crowd liked the town so much is (that) nobody bothered them. The residents then were a different breed of cat. They weren't impressed by the movie crowd." Later the celebrated comedian Jack Benny would often broadcast his famous radio show—then heard by an average of eleven million listeners on NBC—from the stage of the Plaza.

Whether Garbo had any company for her visit to Palm Springs that December is not known, However, it is a matter of record that she spent time in Palm Springs, perhaps that week with the bisexual director Edmund Goulding (Chapter 13), who four years earlier directed her (and John and Lionel Barrymore, Wallace Beery, and Joan Crawford) in *Grand Hotel*, in which she uttered her famous "I vant to be left alone" line.

It is well known that Greta Garbo spent a lot of time in Palm Springs, sometimes under her assumed traveling name of Harriet Brown. One reason was that she had many friends in the resort; in 1939 she stayed there with her friend Gayelord Hauser, the fad nutrionist whose discipline she followed by, among other things, drinking large quantities of carrot juice.

In 1967 her brother, Sven Gustafson, died of a heart attack at Palm Springs Desert Regional Hospital. Whether she was there at the time or not isn't recorded, but it is known that she deeply loved her older brother despite his attempts to cash in on her fame by using "Sven Garbo" as his stage name during his failed film career.

By then, though, Garbo's film career was long past and she had become more or less a recluse in New York City.

She died at eighty-four on April 15, 1990. Her ashes were buried at the Woodland Cemetery in her native Stockholm, Sweden.

# CHAPTER SEVEN

# ROCK AND GEORGE

A couple of generations back, Palm Springs was known for, among other things, being a great place for Hollywood swingers to stash their mistresses (or misters) du jour. Howard Hughes famously boarded a fifteen-year-old starlet in a hotel he owned, which is now a clothing-optional gay resort. It was also a retreat for the stars to dry out, lose weight, or carry on clandestine liaisons with partners of the moment.

It was the sexual freedom that was the most popular draw of Palm Springs and some of the adjoining communities, and it still is for many. Privacy, as was noted earlier, was provided by the ubiquitous walls surrounding many of the community's homes and resorts, yet the place was still close enough to the studios that a star could show up for a movie or television production call in a couple of hours.

So, for the publicly homophobic Liberace (who once sued a British newspaper for saying he was gay while at the same time cavorting with bevies of young male beauties behind the walls of a succession of homes) and hundreds of closeted gay, lesbian, and bisexual actors, actresses, and their friends, a trek to the desert was the ideal solution to having your fame as well as enjoying it. On at least one occasion in the mid-1950s, Tab Hunter and his then boyfriend, Tony Perkins, hid out together at the Desert Inn, where Hunter was often photographed by the fan magazines, provocatively posed on the diving board or in the pool, to satisfy the fantasy of millions of female teens.

It was also in those mid-fifties—November 9, 1955, to be exact—that Rock Hudson, the hottest male star in the country and the very image of the era's wholesome manliness, was forced to marry his agent's secretary to avoid being "outed" by the gossip press. Her name was Phyllis Gates, she was (as later testimony confirmed) a lesbian as promiscuous in her circles as Hudson was in gay circles. She was also well aware of the gay underground through her boss, talent manager Henry Willson, who was famous for making stars of men and women—like Tab Hunter, Natalie Wood, Troy Donahue, Rory Calhoun, Robert Wagner, and Guy Madison—whose looks were sometimes far more obvious than their acting talent. He was also famous for inventing memorable names for his clients as well as demanding sexual favors of the male clients.

Willson maneuvered the Hudson/Gates wedding just in time. A month earlier, the October 3, 1955, issue of *Life* magazine headlined: "Fans are urging 29-year-old Hudson to get married—or explain why not." The potential revelation that actually provoked the wedding was much more dramatic than *Life*'s softball coverage, and to protect Hudson, who was his biggest ticket client of the moment, Willson had no hesitation about throwing two of his other clients under the bus.

Forget all the bad things you've heard about the activities of today's tabloid media; they amount to nothing compared with the reputation of *Confidential* in the 1950s, a magazine that was notorious for revealing sordid details of the stars' private lives when they were considered far more scandalous than today (founded in 1952, *Confidential* pioneered reportage of scandal, gossip, and exposé, in a mixture that *Newsweek* described as "sin and sex with a seasoning of right-wing politics"). In the late summer of 1955 *Confidential*'s editors—not surprisingly, since they blackmailed Hollywood talent all the time—reportedly contacted Willson and threatened to publish an exposé about Hudson's secret homosexual life unless he gave them enough dirt on his other clients. Willson apparently did so, disclosing private information about Rory Calhoun's years in prison (as a juvenile delinquent) and Tab Hunter's arrest at a so-called gay pajama party in 1950. The writing was on the wall: Rock Hudson had to get married.

As an example of the kind of Hollywood journalism that makes even the most credible viewer of Hollywood's opportunism more than a little cynical, when Phyllis Gates died of lung cancer in January 2006, the *Los Angeles Times* remembered her in an obituary that was, infamously, far longer than those of many famous stars. It also portrayed her as a devoted wife who was duped by a deceitful employer into marrying a promiscuous gay man to protect his reputation (and her boss's business). This, despite the fact that many Hollywood insiders and, presumably, *Los Angeles Times* writers, columnists, and editors knew that she was a lesbian who, from the time she started working for Willson, couldn't help but know that Hudson was gay. She never remarried during the forty-eight years remaining to her after the couple's divorce in 1958.

"Phyllis had a double standard," Hudson's longtime friend and secretary, Mark Miller, once said of the marriage. "That is: She could go out with women, but Hudson couldn't [date] men. Always the pragmatist, Phyllis feared that Hudson's homosexuality would be exposed and, in effect, derail her gravy train as 'Mrs. Star.'"

In April 1958 Gates filed for divorce, citing "mental cruelty," but in some ways the trouble was just beginning. "Gates received a relatively small alimony of $250 a week for ten years," the *L.A. Times* obit stated, while not seeing fit to mention the car, the wedding gifts, and Rock Hudson's house on Warbler Place in Hollywood, worth $32,000 in 1950s dollars (maybe half a million dollars today), that she also received.

According to another Willson client, actor Paul Nesbitt, the agent actually ordered up a mob hit either to rough up or to rub out two individuals who were blackmailing Rock with evidence of his gay sexual activities (supplied by Gates,) and threatening to go to the tabloids. Willson also made sure the mob also paid a visit to Gates. Apparently she didn't understand; not long afterward Willson and Hudson had to acquire incriminating photos of Gates' own carryings-on in order to shut her up a second time. (The episode is recorded as a blind item in gossip maven Liz Smith's autobiography, *Natural Blonde*.)

Having developed a taste for extortion, Gates turned to other women but was no more successful prying money out of her own sex. On one occasion when Gates tried to blackmail a wealthy woman with whom she had had an affair, the effort fizzled; it turned out that the woman didn't care whether or not her husband (who was gay) found out about her extramarital liaison with Gates.

The *L.A. Times* nevertheless quoted Gates in their obit as once saying: "I had the power to destroy Rock and I didn't use it. To have exposed his other life would have been vicious and vindictive. I faced enough trouble rebuilding my life without bearing that guilt." The paper also left out any mention of Phyllis's various female partners or the story that shortly before her death she was named as correspondent with another woman in a divorce suit filed by the husband.

When Hudson capitulated to marriage, the news, appropriately enough, was made known to the world by the major film fan magazines. One story, headlined "When Day Is Done, Heaven Is Waiting," quoted Hudson as saying, "When I count my blessings, my marriage tops the list." The marriage and the way it was publicized was, like Hudson's straight, he-man public image, a typical coverup in that era of denial. And for some reason, there still exists hypocrisy over Rock Hudson's private life. Recently one of Hudson's closest friends and professional associates who is openly gay claimed to the writer: "I don't think Rock spent much time in Palm Springs," despite the fact that, as was well known at the time, the desert resort was central to much of Hudson's sexual activity. And in 1990 when Hollywood publicist Tom Clark, Hudson's live-in lover for at least a decade, published *Rock Hudson, Friend of Mine*, he sanitized their relationship, never once admitting that the pair were lovers.

Rock Hudson was born Roy Harold Scherer Jr., in Winnetka, Illinois, on November 17, 1925, the son of Katherine Wood, a telephone operator, and Roy Harold Scherer Sr., a hard-drinking auto mechanic who abandoned the family during the depths of the Great Depression in the early 1930s. His mother remarried, and his stepfather Wallace "Wally" Fitzgerald, adopted him, changing his last name to Fitzgerald. Hudson's years at New Trier High School were unremarkable. He sang in the school's glee club and was remembered as a shy boy who delivered newspapers, ran errands, and worked as a golf caddy. His favorite reading at the time, however, was the fan magazine *Photoplay*.

After graduating from high school, he served in the Philippines as an aircraft mechanic for the U.S. Navy during World War II. In 1946 the twenty-one-year-old Roy Fitzgerald moved to Los Angeles to pursue an acting career and applied to the University of Southern California's dramatics program but was rejected for his earlier poor grades.

To support himself, Roy worked as a truck driver for a couple years, but, probably remembering old *Photoplay* overnight success stories, spent most of his time passing out head shots to people entering the studio's gates. In 1948 he was "discovered" by Henry Willson, who changed his name (for some reason, said to be a combination of the Rock of Gibraltar and the Hudson River—go figure), had his teeth capped, and got him his start in the film business. There is another story that won't go away, one that relates that Roy/Rock-to-be occasionally made deliveries in the Palm Springs area and would often stop off for a little R&R at a then popular gay sex resort in Cathedral City. It is even rumored that it was there that he met Henry Willson, not, as most biographers claim, either while delivering a package to Willson's office or at a party given by the Selznick agent Ken Hodges, Rock's lover and apartment-mate at the time.

Despite Rock's determination to be an actor, at first, it was an uphill fight; in fact, at least one observer commented that the former sailor and truck driver barely knew how to walk in front of a camera. His film debut was as an uncredited U.S. Army Air Force second lieutenant in the 1948 Warner Brothers' film *Fighter Squadron*, and he needed thirty-eight takes before successfully delivering his single line in the film: "You've got to get a bigger blackboard." In his nervousness, it kept coming out, "You've got to get a bligger backboard." Hudson would later recall that, when he took his mother to see the movie, after seeing his one scene, her only comment was, "Save your money."

Obviously more work than just capping teeth was demanded, so Willson, with whom Hudson was apparently also involved sexually, saw to it that Hudson was further coached in acting (including "butching up" his public image), as well as in singing, dancing, fencing, and horseback riding. All the while, the agent was ginning up features touting Hudson's romantic good looks in the fan magazines.

Success and recognition came in 1954 with *Magnificent Obsession*, in which Hudson starred opposite the popular Jane Wyman as a bad boy who is redeemed. The film received rave reviews, and *Modern Screen Magazine* hailed Hudson as the most popular actor of the year. In 1956 his popularity exploded when he starred as Jordan Benedict, the heir to one of the largest cattle ranching families in Texas, in *Giant.* Based on Edna Ferber's novel, the hugely successful, Oscar-winning epic directed by George Stevens co-starred Elizabeth Taylor and James Dean. Dean and Hudson were both nominated for Oscars; sadly it was a second posthumous nomination for Dean, who died September 30, 1955, in a car crash near Salinas, California. (Dean's other posthumous nomination was for his performance in *East of Eden.*) As most film fans remember, Dean was driving a limited edition Porsche 550 when he hit a truck and was killed near Salinas, California. The car, incidentally, had recently been bought to replace the Porsche 356 Speedster in which he came in second in the Palm Springs Road Races the previous March and subsequently raced in Bakersfield and Santa Monica before trading it for the more powerful 550.

•••••

A generation later Hudson's life trajectory was to end far differently, but as tragically.

Following 1957's *Something of Value,* and a moving performance in 1957's *A Farewell to Arms,* based on Ernest Hemingway's novel (Hudson turned down the role of Messala, Charlton Heston's *Ben Hur* rival, to make the Hemingway film; he later claimed it was the biggest mistake of his professional life), his reputation would be made over the next decade with a series of romantic comedies. They are also the films in which most fans remember him today and include *Pillow Talk,* the first of several successful films in which he co-starred with Doris Day. It was followed by *Come September, Send Me No Flowers, Man's Favorite Sport?* and *Strange Bedfellows.*

Hudson's movie popularity diminished after the decade of the sixties, and, like his friend and near-exact contemporary Robert Wagner (whose early career, as was earlier noted, was also managed by Henry Willson), the actor successfully segued from film to television, starring most famously in the NBC series *McMillan and Wife* from 1971 to 1977, co-starring with Susan Saint James.

A generation earlier Hudson made a rare pre-*McMillan and Wife* television appearance in an April 1955 episode of the biggest show on television, *I Love Lucy.* It was a testament both to Hudson's tremendous early popularity at the time and to his identification with Palm Springs (he reportedly told the producers that if they wanted him, it would have to be filmed on his turf). In the episode titled "In Palm Springs," Lucy and her pal Ethel (Vivian Vance) take a trip to the desert playground without their husbands to escape marital boredom, the highlight of which is meeting Rock Hudson.

After Hudson and Gates divorced, he was seen in the company of several good-looking young men. One of them was his friend George Nader, who became the life partner of the actor's secretary, Mark Miller. Nader had a weekend place in Bermuda Dunes, some 25 miles southeast of Palm Springs, and occasionally took Hudson water-skiing at the Salton Sea. So close were Hudson, Nader, and Miller that Hudson's biographer, Sara Davidson, described the couple as "Rock's family for most of his adult life."

When Hudson died of AIDS in 1985, he left Nader and Miller a large part of his $28 million estate. Notoriously, the will was contested by Hudson's former lover, Marc Christian, who claimed that Hudson hid the fact that he had AIDS while still indulging in unprotected sex with him; this was red meat for the tabloids. After a long battle, Nader and Miller received $5.5 million, which allowed the couple to live in luxury in Palm Springs in the upscale Vista Las Palmas neighborhood..

Born in Pasadena, California, on October 9, 1921, George Nader, earned a B.A. in theater arts at Occidental College and spent four years at the famed Pasadena Playhouse, during which time he also served as a U.S. Navy communications officer. It wasn't long before the handsome actor caught Hollywood's eye, and he made his screen debut as an American airman who falls in love with a Swedish girl in 1949's *Memory of Love*. This role was an exception, though; in the beginning most of his early roles were small, uncredited parts in major films such as 1951's *Two Tickets to Broadway* (which starred Tony Martin and Janet Leigh) and the same year's *Take Care of My Little Girl* (with Jeanne Crain, Dale Robertson, and Mitzi Gaynor), or larger ones in movies such as 1953's *Sins of Jezebel*, one of Paulette Goddard's last films. His first starring role was in that year's 3-D film *Robot Monster*; filmed in Hollywood's Bronson Canyon in four days for $16,000 and considered one of the worst movies ever made, it nevertheless earned more than a million dollars. Nader's career was on its way.

Universal put him in a Rory Calhoun western, *Four Guns to the Border* (1954) and gave him the key role of a cop who takes a paternal interest in a juvenile delinquent (Tony Curtis) in *Six Bridges to Cross* (1955). He received a Golden Globe award as "the most promising newcomer of 1954" and was then given a role opposite Jeanne Crain—this time as a leading man and not an uncredited actor—in 1955's *The Second Greatest Sex*, a musical western (of all bad ideas!). Before his Hollywood career ended, Nader starred with Jeff Chandler in *Away All Boats* (1956), and with Esther Williams in *The Unguarded Moment* (1956), Julie Adams in *Four Girls in Town* (1957), and Phyllis Thaxter in 1957's *Man Afraid*. In 1958's *The Female Animal*, he played a film extra lusted after by both a fading film star (Hedy Lamarr) and her daughter (Jane Powell). Like Hudson, Nader was publicized as dating a bevy of Hollywood stars and starlets, among them Joan Crawford, but his heart wasn't in it.

The problem wasn't Hedy Lamarr's lusting over the hunky Nader (who had a side career as a beefcake model by keeping fit through swimming and weightlifting); it was Rock Hudson. Sal Mineo, who made his film debut playing Tony Curtis's character as a boy in *Six Bridges to Cross*, once said that he was surprised at the open homosexual affairs going on in Hollywood at the time (1954), one of the most prominent being the relationship between Nader and Rock Hudson. It was too blatant and, again, *Confidential* was the catalyst for another scandal coverup.

The magazine threatened to publish the details of Nader's relationship with Rock Hudson (despite the fact that by then Nader was seriously involved with Mark Miller) and, according to Hollywood underground skinny at the time, Universal cut a deal with the magazine and agreed to fire Nader if the information about Hudson was suppressed. Nader fled to Europe, where he made a number of films including a series of German action thrillers, playing an FBI agent named Jerry Cotton—not long ago a staple of German late night television.

•••••

After Nader returned to Los Angeles, his eye was seriously injured in a car accident in the mid-seventies, and he turned to writing. *Chrome*, his first book, published in 1978, was a highly praised science fiction novel about a gay romance between a man and a robot. *The Perils of Paul*, set in Hollywood's gay community, would not, at his request, be published until after his death (there is no record that it ever was published).

George Nader died from a bacterial infection on February 4, 2002. He was, as his friend Tony Curtis said, "one of the kindest and most generous men I've ever known." The actor Michael Nader is his nephew.

In the early 1980s, after years of heavy drinking and smoking, Rock Hudson began having health problems. Emergency quintuple heart bypass surgery in November 1981 sidelined the actor and his new television show, *The Devlin Connection*, for a year. (The show was cancelled soon after it returned to NBC.) As Hudson had done while recuperating from earlier illnesses, after the operation he spent much of his recovery time in Palm Springs, where he stayed with Miller and Nader.

In 1984, in part because producers Aaron Spelling and Richard and Esther Shapiro knew he was ill and wanted work, Hudson was given the plum role of Linda Evans' sometime love interest in the hit ABC prime-time soap *Dynasty*. From the very beginning of his career, as we have seen, Hudson had trouble memorizing lines; on *Dynasty*, his speech itself began to deteriorate. In July 1985 Hudson joined his old friend Doris Day for the launch of her new TV cable show, *Doris Day's Best Friends*. His gaunt visage and his nearly incoherent speech were so shocking that clips from the show were rebroadcast on national news broadcasts for weeks to come.

Hudson had been diagnosed with HIV on June 5, 1984, but when the signs of illness became apparent, his publicity people and doctors lied and told the public he had liver cancer. It was not until July 25, 1985, while Hudson was in Paris for treatment after Doris Day's show was broadcast, that his publicist announced that he was dying of AIDS. Hudson later claimed that he might have contracted the disease through blood from an infected donor during the multiple blood transfusions he received as part of his 1981 heart bypass operation.

He was flown back to Los Angeles on July 31 on a chartered

Air France Boeing 747, and he spent a month at Cedars Sinai Hospital undergoing further treatment. When it became clear that there was no hope of saving his life, Hudson returned to his home, where he remained in seclusion until his death on October 2. He was fifty-nine years old.

Unlike Doris Day, who claimed after his death that she never knew he was gay, Carol Burnett, who often worked on television and live theater with Hudson, was a staunch defender of her friend, telling an interviewer that she knew about his sexuality and did not care.

The actress Morgan Fairchild said, "Rock Hudson's death gave AIDS a face."

CHAPTER EIGHT

# TAB

"I hate labels" are the very first words in Tab Hunter's 2005 tell-all memoir, *Tab Hunter, Confidential,* in which he traced his amazing rise and fall from obscurity to one of the biggest box office attractions in movie history in the mid-1950s.

He's referring to such labels as "the sigh guy," one of the terms coined by the movie fan magazines to describe his tremendous popularity with millions of teen girls who lusted after him at the time. But he also is referring to the term "gay." Although he never hid from friends and colleagues the fact that he was gay, he first spoke about it publicly in his book, in which he also revealed a longtime relationship with Anthony Perkins, famed for, among many roles, playing the eerie Norman Bates in Alfred Hitchcock's 1960 suspense/horror film *Psycho* and its three sequels. He also describes liaisons with the legendary dancer Rudolf Nureyev, actor Scott Marlowe (who resembled Tab's friend James Dean in appearance as well as acting style), and ice skater Ronnie Robertson.

His relationship with the late Tony Perkins, before only rumored, lasted several years. "Everyone seems to want to know why it ended," he says today. "We just outgrew each other," he explains, instantly adding to qualify the clichéd excuse. "We were apart a lot of the time. I was off making movies. He was off in Australia for a long time making *On the Beach* (1958). That's the real story of what happened." Perkins, who died of complications from AIDS in 1992, married photographer Berry Berenson in 1973 when he was forty-one and fathered two children.

•••••

Speaking from his home in Montecito, California (a suburb of Santa Barbara), which he shares today with his younger partner of twenty-five years, film producer Allen Glaser, he says of the gay world—or at least the gay world as it was fifty years ago: "I always felt uncomfortable with it."

Nevertheless for the 1950s and much of the next decade, Tab considered Palm Springs and its environs a second home, a place to which he escaped weekend after weekend, but usually in the company of straight friends and aspiring actors, both male and female. "I even remember when they planted the palm trees on Palm Canyon (Drive)," he laughs. "Going to Palm Springs was never a big thing....it was a place where all of us could get together and have a wonderful time on weekends.

"Sometimes we'd get gussied up and go out to the Chi-Chi [a famous club of the era] or the Doll's House [an equally famous restaurant]. And I'd realize 'There's Lana [Turner], there's Frank [Sinatra], or there's Ava [Gardner].'"

And, hard as it may be to believe, as far as he remembers, he and Tony Perkins apparently visited the desert resort only once during their lengthy relationship, when they stayed at the

Lois Kellogg (Chapter 3) with one of her famous Russian Wolfhounds in the early 1920s. *Credit: Palm Springs Historical Society.*

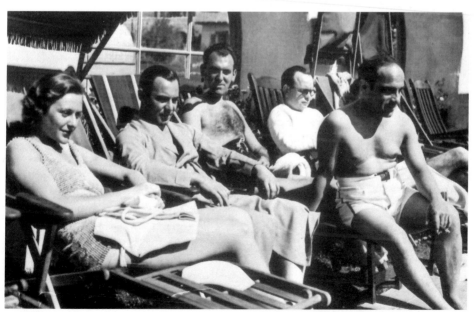

Relaxing at the pool of the El Mirador hotel in the late 1950: (L to R) Dorothy and Richard Rodgers, Moss Hart, longtime Twentieth Century Fox publicity director Harry Brand, and, in front, Lorenz Hart (Chapter 14). *Credit: Palm Springs Historical Society.*

Betsy Drake and Cary Grant ca. 1959 at Palm Springs' Smoke Tree Ranch where they often rode horseback during their marriage (Chapter 4). *Credit: Palm Springs Historical Society.*

Liberace in the kitchen of Casa Liberace. He is joined by his business manager (probably Clarence Goodwin) who was a very busy man during this period of the mid-1950s when the entertainer was earning over a million dollars a year (Chapter 9). *Credit: Palm Springs Historical Society.*

Claudette Colbert reaches for a ball at the El Mirador resort in 1932 (Chapter 6). *Credit: Palm Springs Historical Society.*

Mary Martin and Palm Springs mayor Frank Bogert at Palm Springs' Flower Drum Restaurant in the late 1980s. They were joined by dancer Kitty Ito and restaurant owner Peter Lee (Chapter 11). *Credit: Palm Springs Historical Society.*

Rudolph Valentino photographed during a visit with the then-famous Palm Springs "hermit" William Pester (who, infamously at the time, wore clothes only when he expected guests), ca. 1921 (Chapter 2). *Credit: Palm Springs Historical Society.*

Dr. Florilla White (right) and Rose Dougan on a desert horseback ride in February 1934 (Chapter 2). *Credit: Palm Springs Historical Society.*

(L to R) Director Edmund Goulding (Chapter 13), Greta Garbo, and John Gilbert on the set of 1927's *Love.* Only months later, Gilbert was stood up at the altar by Garbo, as related in Chapter 6. *Credit: Palm Springs Historical Society.*

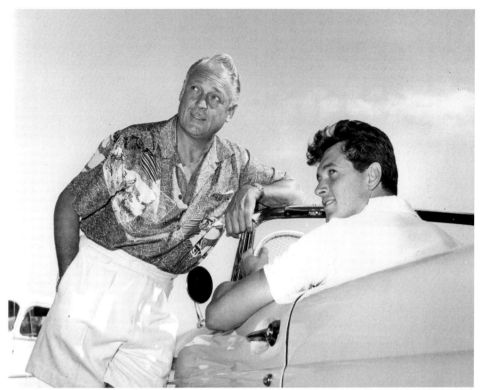

Something (or someone) clearly caught the attention of former silent film star Charles Farrell—by then a TV star and mayor of Palm Springs—and Rock Hudson one autumn day in Palm Springs in 1955 (Chapters 7 and 10). *Credit: Bill Augerson.*

Tab Hunter larking with a bevy of young movie hopefuls filling his first "movie star" car, a 1953 "Flamingo Red" Ford convertible during a *Photoplay* shoot in Palm Springs in the fall of 1954. They include (l to r), Brett Halsey; John Ericson (face obscured); Pat Crowley (being helped out of the car by Tab); Renate Hoy; and Lori Nelson. Both Crowley and Nelson would later guest star on Tab's 1960 NBC series, "The Tab Hunter Show" (Chapter 8). *Credit: Tab Hunter collection.*

Was anyone ever so blond? Tab Hunter poses for a movie fan magazine in the pool of the Desert Inn resort in 1954 (Chapter 8). *Credit: Tab Hunter collection.*

Janet Gaynor and her husband Paul Gregory at their Singing Tree Ranch in Desert Hot Springs in 1983 while Gaynor was recuperating from a near-fatal car accident. She would die the following year from the injuries she sustained. (Chapter 10). *Credit: Palm Springs Historical Society.*

Cheryl Crane and her partner Josh LeRoy, photographed by Greg Gorman at Hollywood's Le Dome restaurant in the late 1990s. Their unlikely escorts were filmmaker John Waters and nightclub singer Michael Feinstein. (Chapter 5). *Credit: Cheryl Crane collection.*

Jeffrey Sanker, founder of Palm Springs famous White Party, billed as the nation's largest gay dance festival (Chapter 1). *Credit: Jeffrey Sanker*

Gay men from around the world fill the pool at Palm Springs' Wyndham Hotel during the White Party weekend every spring (Chapter 1). *Credit: Jeffrey Sanker.*

It looks pretty tame here, but at any moment while exploring the lush landscape of Palm Springs' Vista Grande (clothing optional) resort, you will, more often than not, encounter a group of stark naked men (Chapter 1). *Credit: Vista Grande resort.*

The late Gloria Greene with her ever-present cigarillo at a celebrity "roast" in the 1990s at Palm Springs' famous Streetbar, the first gay business in the Arenas Road gay heart of the city and the longest running gay and lesbian bar in the entire Coachella Valley. Since opening in 1991 as A Streetbar Named Desire, its staff and customers have, following Greene's example, raised over $200,000 for local, primarily AIDS related, charities (Chapter 13). *Credit: Richard Hascamp.*

Desert Inn in 1956 or 1957. "We often weekended at Lake Ar-
rowhead, where I taught Tony to water ski," Tab recalls. For
most of the time he spent in Palm Springs over the course of
two decades, he stayed with friends, friends like Harold Lloyd Jr.,
son of the great silent comic; antique dealer Paul Ferrante, and
Joan Harvey, who was married to Columbia Pictures boss Harry
Cohn from 1941 until his death in 1958 and later was the wife of
actor Laurence Harvey. "I passed a kidney stone at Joan's house,"
Tab recalls with a laugh.

Part of the reason for Tab's reluctance to become identified
with the gay life in Palm Springs, or Hollywood for that matter,
was the closeted attitudes of the pre-Stonewall era in which he
was raised in the Roman Catholic faith by a conservative mother
who always cautioned him to "stay quiet, don't draw attention to
yourself, be discreet."

At the time, homosexuality was for many still a subject beyond the pale of polite conversation or understanding. This was
to an extent true even in Palm Springs—at least in public—
which then as now had a larger than average population of gay
and lesbians because of the proximity of Hollywood talent, a
large percentage of which was gay, lesbian, or bisexual. Even
mentioning the subject was "Like having bad breath," Tab recalls. "It was something you never talked about."

Another reason for Tab's reticence is that he was, and remains, a very private person. Such a passion for privacy as his
could hardly fail to have been fostered by the relentless battle
between the tabloid media, determined to "out" him when he became famous, and his studio, determined to protect the straight-
arrow, boy-next-door image of one of their biggest stars.

His career was seriously challenged even before it got a start
when, at eighteen, a gay "slumber party" in a Los Angeles suburb was raided only moments after he arrived and he, along with
everyone else, was hauled off to jail. The fact that it wasn't a "pa-

jama" party or that he apparently didn't know what he was get-
ting into when he was arrested (he eventually was charged with
"disorderly conduct " and fined $50) didn't count. It was enough
to scare anyone deep into the closet. Then in September 1955,
right on the heels of his first huge success in the film *Battle Cry*,
there appeared, prominently displayed on the newsstands next to
the movie magazines headlining the expected puff pieces about
his "straight" lifestyle and purported girlfriends, was the notorious 4.5-million-circulation *Confidential* magazine with a ban-
ner blaring: "The Lowdown on that Disorderly Conduct Charge
against Tab Hunter." Inside, the story described how some five
years earlier he was hauled off to jail " in a paddy wagon with a
load of shrill nances." The revelation in fact was another example of Hollywood loyalty: for the magazine to kill a story about
Rock Hudson's gay carryings-on, Hunter's former agent gave it
Tab's "pajama party" story as well as one about Rory Calhoun's
adolescent run-in with the law.

So, if Tab was earlier unable to relax into his gay being even
in the then reasonably tolerant Palm Springs of the 1950s, the
pressure to keep a lid on his private life would only mount as his
career exploded, crowned by his performance in the 1958 Warner Brothers' film *Damn Yankees.*

Of Tab's performance, the film's director Stanley Donen ob-
served: "He couldn't sing, he couldn't dance, he couldn't act. He
was a triple threat."

By that time, buoyed by the tremendous audience response to
his earlier appearances in films, the blond, boyish actor had become the number one male teen heartthrob in the country. One
of his early movies, *Island of Desire*, set during World War II on
a deserted tropical South Seas isle, introduced another aspect to
Tab's fame: the fact that his shirt remained off for a good por-
tion of the film did not go unnoticed by his ever-growing legion
of female—and male—fans. Images of his face and bare chest

were to become a standard studio publicity department cliché of the time and seemingly thereafter; one was chosen to adorn the cover of Donald Reuter's 2001 book, *Shirtless! The Hollywood Male Physique.*

•••••

A year before the release of *Damn Yankees,* Tab had parlayed his booming popularity into making pop records, several of which made the charts. The most famous, "Young Love" (on Dot Records), shot to number one worldwide in 1957 (knocking Elvis out of the top spot) and remained there for weeks. On its flip side was Tab's nearly as popular rendition of the older song "Red Sails in the Sunset."

Put it all together, and what Donen was really saying about Tab was that what he was able to bring to *Damn Yankees* was far more important than his acting or singing or dancing talent. By that point in his career—he was then twenty-seven—he brought to the film, and many more to follow, the same intangible something that, say, Elizabeth Taylor, could deliver in her prime: an immense star power.

In addition to "the sigh guy" moniker, Tab was also referred to as "date bait," and the "All American Boy" by fan magazines such as *Photoplay, Modern Screen,* and *Movieland,* which shot many of their layouts featuring the star in Palm Springs. "Hollywood's Most Eligible Bachelor" was constantly linked with female stars, as were many other gay actors at the time including, as we have seen, Rock Hudson. Among them was Natalie Wood, Hunter's co-star in 1956's *The Burning Hills* and *The Girl He Left Behind.* Both World War II war films, they were among many made by Hunter, who appeared on screen in military uniforms far more than he was seen shirtless. "I should have been on the government's payroll," he laughs these days.

Tab was born Arthur Andrew Kelm in New York City on July 11, 1931, the younger of two sons of Charles Kelm and Gertrude Gelien (his older brother, Walt, died in Vietnam in October 1965). After divorcing his abusive father, Tab's mom, Gertrude, moved the children to California and changed their last name to her maiden name of Gelien. Eventually they ended up in the Los Angeles area, moving from apartment to apartment, a pattern Tab replicated in the early days of his career.

Tab left school when he was fifteen and joined the Coast Guard (he lied about his age and was discharged when his real age was discovered). Earlier, when he was twelve (but passing for fourteen), a rising actor named Dick Clayton met him and, after the Coast Guard episode, introduced him to Henry Willson, then a superagent who was famed for inventing memorable names for his male clientele (some of whom, we said earlier, he also had sexual relationships with, but, apparently, not Tab). Willson came up with Tab ("We have to tab you with something," he said) and Hunter (because of the young actor's love of horses). Clayton, sixteen years older than Tab, would become an agent himself and represent Hunter for years. They also became close buddies. "He was like a brother," Tab adds. "He was my confidant."

In the late 1950s Clayton bought five acres of homestead land off the Palm to Pines highway in Palm Desert, a thriving community near Palm Springs, for a price that makes people today wince: $5.00. Having homestead land means that you have to build something on it, and Tab and Clayton—often assisted by other aspiring actors and actresses, including John Ericson and Lori Nelson, all sleeping in sleeping bags under the desert stars—built a cinder block cottage.

With no previous experience Tab made his first, albeit minor, film debut in 1950's racially driven drama *The Lawless*, which starred Gail Russell and Macdonald Carey. Unlike the case with

Rock Hudson, whose one line in his first film required thirty-eight takes, Tab's line was simply cut.

Obviously it didn't matter, since Tab's ability to deliver lines was less than important than his physique. In his next film, the British-made *Saturday Island* (also called *Island of Desire*) (1952), he co-starred with the decade-older Linda Darnell. It was optioned by Warner Brothers, and Tab's stardom was clinched in 1955 with the release of another World War II epic, *Battle Cry*, based on the Leon Uris novel. In the film he again played a boyish soldier sharing torrid scenes with an older woman—this time Dorothy Malone, playing a love-starved Navy wife. (In the summer of 1956 Warner re-released *Battle Cry* as a double bill with *East of Eden* starring Hunter's late friend James Dean and Julie Harris; it was billed as a package starring the country's "two top actors of the year.")

Reportedly, Jack Warner originally planned to cast Tab and his friend Debbie Reynolds instead of Dean and Natalie Wood in his next film *Rebel Without a Cause*; considering the fact that Dean, Wood, and co-star Sal Mineo all died under tragic circumstances, maybe Warner unknowingly did Hunter a favor. Also, right up among Hollywood's most improbable casting stories is the screen test Tab made to star opposite Liberace in the pianist's 1955 film *Sincerely Yours* (Tab was rejected for looking too young). As he recalls: "What a concept—the most extravagantly effeminate man in Hollywood teamed with the all-American boy. What is even more outrageous is that in 1954 [when the film was made], the majority of the public had no idea that either of us was gay. [It] would be considered some sort of camp classic today."

Although his singing career was brief, its success provided the justification—despite director Donen's opinion—for Tab's being cast in *Damn Yankees*. Top-billed as baseball fan Joe Hardy in the musical based on the classic Faust legend, he played opposite Gwen Verdon and Ray Walston, who re-created their devil-making Broadway roles (Tab replaced Stephen Douglass, who created the role on Broadway) It would turn out to be the greatest success of Tab's film career.

Also in that year of 1958 he donned a uniform yet again in the William Wellman–directed *Lafayette Escadrille,* playing a wholesome soldier, this time, however, in World War I. (Wellman directed *Wings,* also a World War I aviation drama, which won the first Best Picture Oscar. He also wrote and directed the 1937 version of A *Star Is Born* starring Janet Gaynor, for which he won the Best Screenplay Oscar.) More spicy love scenes came Tab's way with 1959's *That Kind of Woman,* an adult comedy-drama that focused on Hunter and his sexy mistress Sophia Loren.

Despite the determination to sell him as an all-American straight boy—he couldn't do much about those looks and that athletic physique, though; was anyone ever so blond?—Tab remains a big supporter of the studio system despite its abuses of talent. "They took care of you," he says.

Since it has been years since the studio contract system ruled Hollywood, a word is in order about what was the foundation of the film industry for more than a couple of generations, affecting every actor in Hollywood for good and for bad. Shirley MacLaine once called it a "slave trade," and she was hardly the first to do so.

In the past, eight major studios ruled Hollywood, and one of the ways they did so was by discovering, grooming, and then exploiting their own stars, who in turn, would draw audiences to theaters the studios owned or controlled. This system provided security for both the studios and the stars—so long as they behaved—which is one reason the system lasted for a half-century. The studio contracts were normally for seven years, during which, in addition to assigning actors and actresses to whatever films the studio decided, they could also loan them out to another studio for, usually, significantly more money than the actor made. A famous example was Clark Gable, loaned out by MGM to David O. Selznick to star in 1939's *Gone With the Wind*. And of course, as we have seen, after 1934 the actors were required to sign a morals clause that was so stringent that very few human beings could do so without crossed fingers.

Also as part of those contracts, if actors refused to do *anything* the studio desired (including the films they were assigned, the shooting schedule, the locations, etc.), the studio could suspend them indefinitely until they did as ordered—and of course the suspension time was added onto the original contract. Greta Garbo, probably the most famous star in Hollywood's history, was suspended six times by Louis B. Mayer. Tab Hunter was suspended twice by Jack Warner for turning down projects..

In 1959 Tab bought out his Warner contract and paid the price. With no studio to protect him, he was at the mercy of several trumped-up lawsuits, most notoriously one accusing him of beating his pet Weimaraner, a charge that was leveled by a neighbor's teen daughter who was apparently frustrated that Tab wouldn't pay attention to her.

Nevertheless, he continued to make interesting films. Among them was an early television appearance in February 1958, when director Arthur Penn—somewhat surprisingly when one considers the teen audience appeal of Tab's films—chose Tab to co-star with the young Geraldine Page in an episode of television's most respected dramatic series, CBS's *Playhouse 90*. For his performance as the killer in "Portrait of a Murderer," Hunter earned an Emmy nomination. That year he also played against his teen heartthrob image in the movie *Gunman's Walk*, co-starring with veteran Van Heflin and James Darren (who in 1959 would himself achieve teen fame of sorts by playing Moondoggie in *Gidget*).

By then, however, Tab's reign as a teen idol had been eclipsed by Troy Donahue, the new beefcake on the block. With fewer film offers coming his way, the actor switched to television, first with his own series *The Tab Hunter Show* (1960), a light sitcom that centered around his swinging bachelor pad; it lasted only one season—it could hardly do otherwise, airing as it did against the *Ed Sullivan Show*, then one of the most popular shows on television. He would, however, go on to make over 200 television programs, including an ongoing character in *Mary Hartman, Mary Hartman.*

After in a delightful performance opposite Debbie Reynolds in 1961's *The Pleasure of His Company,* Tab's film career hit the skids with films such as *Operation Bikini* (1963), *Ride the Wild Surf* (1964), *The City Under the Sea* (1965), and 1966's *Birds Do It* (1966). In 1964 he was invited to star on Broadway opposite Talullah Bankhead in Tennessee Williams's *The Milk Train Doesn't Stop Here Anymore.* It lasted five performances. Ever the survivor, however, when it looked like his career was going the way of many has-beens, Tab became immensely popular on the dinner club circuit.

And so it continued until 1981, when Tab, spoofing his old clean-cut image, was cast as the romantic fantasy of heavyset transvestite "actress" Divine in the deliriously tasteless (and instantly hip) John Waters film *Polyester.* This film was followed by a role in *Grease 2* (in which, Tab played a biology teacher who, with his students, sings the film's hit song, "Reproduction").

Then he hit pay dirt again. In 1985 he co-starred again with Divine (Tab still calls the late Glenn Milstead, who played Divine, "his favorite actress") in the Western spoof, also an instant cult hit, *Lust in the Dust.* He also coproduced the movie with a young hotshot producer named Allen Glaser, who had become his lover and, as it turned out, life partner. In 1989 Tab coexecutive produced and hosted the cable series *Hollywood on Horses* and three years later, he wrote the story (and starred in) his thirty-second movie, *Dark Horse,* directed by David Hemmings.

In 2003 Tab, then in his early seventies (although he looks a generation younger) bought a small house at Palm Springs' Racquet Club; recently he had to give it up primarily because of the deluge of invitations—now by aging male admirers—showered on a very private man. Also, Tab laughs, "the summers are too hot for me now."

Not much hotter, actually, than in the late 1950s, when Tab and his agent, Dick Clayton, used to visit Palm Springs in the summer and sleep on rubber mattresses in the pool of the otherwise closed Desert Inn resort.

# CHAPTER NINE

# LEE

hen he's in Palm Springs, Tab Hunter, a Roman Catholic, attends Sunday mass at the tiny Our Lady of Solitude church at the corner of Alejo and Belardo roads. Kitty-cornered from the church is a perfect example of the juxtaposition of the sacred and profane that has defined Palm Springs for generations. And just so you can't miss it, a huge wrought iron chandelier marks the house, known as the Casa de Las Cloisters, but more commonly as the Casa Liberace.

It was the house in which the famous entertainer lived longest among the four he owned during the twenty-five years he called the desert resort home. He also owned the houses where his brother George lived and, next door to Casa Liberace, where his mom resided. It was here that he entertained lavishly, cavorted with bevies of young men (and more than two dozen dogs), and where he died of AIDS in 1987. Today the house is owned by a wealthy San Francisco friend of his named Stefan Hemming, who bought the place a couple years after the entertainer's death; no one would touch it for months because of an assumed possibility—incorrect as we know now—of contracting the HIV infection.

Which reminds me of one of the rather weird coincidences that link three of the most famous gay men of the era—all with deep ties to Palm Springs: Rock Hudson, Liberace, and Tab Hunter.

All three became famous in the mid-1950s and remained closeted (largely for professional reasons) for most of their lives. Both Hudson and Liberace—born Wladziu Valentino Liberace in West Allis, Wisconsin, May 16, 1919—were Midwestern boys of the same generation (Rock was six years younger), who died of AIDS within sixteen months of each other. Toward the end of their lives, both were linked with younger men who exploited their love and trust. Marc Christian would sue Hudson's estate, claiming that Hudson had slept with him when he knew he had AIDS, tying up the will's settlement for some time; Scot Thorson, Liberace's chauffeur, bodyguard, and lover, filed a $113 million palimony suit against the entertainer in 1982, claiming, among other things, that he had been promised an annual income of $70,000 for life. Thorson, who had also undergone cosmetic surgery designed to make him look like Liberace, eventually settled the breach-of-contract suit out of court for $95,000.

Tab Hunter and Liberace made their film debuts in the same year, 1950, Tab in *The Lawless*, and Liberace as a honky tonk pianist in the movie *South Sea Sinner*, which starred Shelley Winters. Five years later when Tab's career exploded with *Battle Cry*, Liberace would star in his own film, *Sincerely Yours*, the story of a deaf concert pianist. Even playing a fictional character, Lee dressed up, ordering from the famous Palm Springs haberdasher, Sy Devore, some of his three dozen or so costumes for his unlikely role in the film as a heterosexual concert pianist caught in a love triangle between two ladies, Joanne Dru and Dorothy Malone.

There the similarities end. Rock Hudson went on to a huge film and television film career, and so, to a somewhat lesser extent, so did Tab. When Tab's hit single "Young Love" hit the top of the charts in the mid-1950s, Liberace was already famous as the star of his own television show. That same year (1954) he also wrote a cookbook and, rather astonishingly, at thirty-six, celebrated his twenty-fifth year in show business with a glitzy concert at the Hollywood Bowl and three Royal Command engagements in England.

That year the then-powerful gossip columnist Cassandra, of the *London Daily Mirror* tabloid newspaper (his real name was William Neil Connor) implied that Liberace was a homosexual in a column; by then, of course, it was the worst-kept secret in show business. Liberace sued and, to the vast amusement of his many gay friends and sexual playmates, won $22,400. "I cried all the way to the bank," he quipped, coining a familiar catchphrase.

Liberace, known to all his friends as Lee, would remain popular with his vast audience for more than a generation. His television show ran on NBC and in syndication from 1952 until 1955, followed by shows on CBS and ABC in the 1960s and 1970s. In the spring of 1984 he returned to New York for an engagement at New York's famed Radio City Music Hall. It broke all sales and attendance records of the fifty-one-year history of the Art Deco palace, with more than 80,000 people buying tickets for what Liberace described as "the fulfillment of a dream and the culmination of my forty years in show business." Commenting on the engagement, the *Wall Street Journal* said: "Liberace occupies his own special rhinestone-studded niche in the American dream."

Nevertheless, for all of his long career, Liberace was looked down on by most serious music lovers. To them, his "tarting up" piano classics to make them more accessible for his basically pop music audience was unforgivable, and he was also seen as degrading the dignity of the classical musician with his costumes and props, which over time became more and more outrageous and, eventually, defined "camp" itself.

In fact, Liberace was actually a child prodigy and a very serious musician born to an equally serious musical family. His father, Salvatore, played French horn in John Philip Sousa's concert band as well as in the Milwaukee Symphony Orchestra and occasionally picked up money as a laborer to keep the family going. But instead of following in his father's footsteps and playing horn, as Salvatore hoped, young Wladziu decided to play piano, at which he turned out to be exceptionally gifted. No less a figure than the world-famous pianist Ignace Jan Paderewski was captivated by his talent; Paderewski, by the way, in addition to being a pianist, was also a composer and in the year 1919 was prime minister of his native Poland, during which time he signed the Versailles Peace Treaty on behalf of his country. The pianist also fostered Liberace's conviction that he was the artistic heir to the legendary, nineteenth-century Hungarian pianist Franz Lizst, and his enthusiastic praise of his protégé was instrumental in securing a scholarship for the seven-year-old Liberace at the Wisconsin College of Music. Lee kept his scholarship for seventeen years, the longest period of time in the history of the academy. When he was eleven, Liberace debuted as a concert soloist in Milwaukee, an event he always considered as the beginning of his professional career. By the time he was sixteen, he was performing with major orchestras, including the prestigious Chicago Symphony.

•••••

In 1940 the twenty-one-year-old pianist moved to New York City, where he took elocution lessons to lessen his Polish accent and began entertaining in nightclubs. In no time he was engaged as an intermission pianist at the world-famous Persian Room of New York's Plaza Hotel. Seven years later he returned to the club as the headliner, complete with his soon-to-be familiar oversize grand piano on which was perched a glittering candelabra—later Liberace's world-famous trademark; reportedly he "discovered" the use of the chandelier when he saw the 1945 film about Chopin, *A Song to Remember*, which starred Cornel Wilde as the pianist and Merle Oberon as George Sand. On the advice of Paderewski, he also dropped his first two names and was billed as simply "Liberace." Thus was born the phenomenon who for much of a generation was known as "Mr. Showmanship" and for a time was also the world's highest paid musician.

During World War II Liberace played with a number of overseas entertainment units, and on his return he continued playing in New York clubs. It wasn't long, however, before he got in trouble with the powerful musicians' union: after he started playing live counterpoints to records broadcast over clubs' sound systems, the union banned him from appearing in New York. Undaunted, he moved to Los Angeles, where he was first considered a potential big band leader like Benny Goodman. But then he signed a record contract with Columbia, and there, under the direction of Mitch Miller, he made a highly emotional version of the Kurt Weill/Maxwell Anderson classic *September Song*. When it was released with a live concert program, it brought his name to a national audience.

Then fate stepped in. While he was playing at the Circus Room night club in the Del Coronado Hotel in San Diego, a television producer named Don Federson heard him and although the show was poorly attended, was impressed enough with his ability to connect with an audience to create a television show featuring the pianist as a summer replacement for Dinah Shore's show. The fifteen-minute, weekly show debuted in 1952 and, because of his glitzy arrangements (and by then, glitzy outfits), it attracted a large national audience. The next year NBC introduced *The Liberace Show*, a weekly half-hour program that made his name a household word and earned him two Emmys.

In 1952, the year his television show premiered, Liberace bought the first of his houses in Palm Springs. "Some people collect stamps," he said in an interview. "I like to collect real estate." All of them reflected his penchant for the gaudy that was so much a part of his professional fame. So was eclecticism: He would mix with abandon French Provincial, Louis XIV, and Art Deco with fake Greek and Roman sculpture. Needless to say, much of the furniture was gaudy and overdecorated; it all looked something like a Russian Baroque palace's furnishings gone mad.

As time went on, Lee's costumes became gaudier and gaudier—some weighed as much as 300 pounds. His jewelry was also so over the top that even the pianist himself made fun of it. "People ask how I can play with all those rings," he said, "and I reply, 'Very well, thank you.'" But his audiences loved it all, anticipating what crazy outfit he would next appear in, hearing about all his houses, his swimming pool shaped like a piano (and at one of his first houses in Palm Springs, also a mailbox), his ornate automobiles, and his exotic dogs and paintings.

Clearly Liberace so obviously enjoyed the glitz and glitter of his public persona that even when he, like Elvis Presley toward the end of his career, appeared as almost a caricature of himself, his sincerity and self-directed jokes disarmed criticism from his millions of fans. In 1955 Liberace, who first performed in Las Vegas a decade earlier, opened at the Riviera Hotel as the highest-paid entertainer in the city's history. (By then he was making a million dollars a year from personal appearances and far more from record sales.) In the 1970s and early 1980s, Liberace's live shows were major box office attractions at the Las Vegas Hilton in Las Vegas and at Lake Tahoe, where he would earn $300,000 a week. He maintained homes in both places.

In 1967 Liberace bought Casa de Las Cloisters, the last of his Palm Springs homes. The seven-bedroom, 8,000-square-foot Spanish-style estate actually started out as a much smaller place when it was built in 1930 by Alvah Hicks, a real estate developer and owner of the local water company. Over the succeeding decades it was expanded by a series of owners and was finally remodeled in 1960 by the famous architect Wallace Neff (whose Hollywood clients included Louis B. Mayer, Charlie Chaplin, and Douglas Fairbanks Jr.) as a boutique hotel complete with a bell tower and wishing wells. The hotel folded six years later and Liberace bought it for $185,000. Rechristening it the Casa de Liberace, he spent $136,000 restoring it, not to its former glory, as most restorers of older homes might do, but as an over-the-top memorial to his own flamboyant taste.

Take, for example, the "Marie Antoinette Room," which boasted pink silk damask wall coverings, or the Safari Room with its African theme, or the Valentino Room (Liberace's memorial to the actor, since his middle name was Valentino), which contained what purportedly was the Latin Lover's own sleigh bed, rescued from Falcon Lair, Valentino's last home. Off the huge pool (added during the 1960 renovation) is the Persian Room, which, it was said at the time, was for hosting orgies with Liberace cavorting naked with teenage French boys. Off the family room (converted from the garage and the room where Liberace died), is a bathroom where the toilet was a throne and the toilet seat still there is made of clear plastic in which are embedded silver and gold coins. The wallpaper, at least until recently, depicted, as the *New York Times* reported, "ancient Greek revelers engaged in a variety of—ahem—ancient Greek activities." There was someone on staff whose entire job was to pick up after the entertainer's eighteen or two dozen or more dogs, depending on who is doing the remembering. "But I still had to replace all the carpets," Hemming has said.

According to Hemming, his furniture—there was hardly a piece that wasn't as over the top as Liberace's—fit into the house "perfectly." One decorating detail that Liberace would certainly have loved had he thought of it: in every room of the house (including halls), among seemingly dozens of paintings, there is always a portrait of Stefan Hemming.

The big event at the house in Liberace's time was his annual Christmas party, which—until a rather gross display was turned on nearby a few years back (reportedly involving six million lights and costing several thousand dollars a night to illuminate)—was the most ostentatious holiday display the town had ever experienced. For example, there were eighteen Christmas trees scattered in and around the estate; the decorations cost $25,000 each year and had to be delivered by moving van.

This was no gay event however—far from it. All Liberace's stagehands and servants and their families were invited to a celebration, and everyone received lavish presents. And on Christmas day itself, after being serenaded by a church choir singing carols, sixteen to eighteen guests sat down to dinner in the large dining room, where the table, today lorded over by a picture of Hemming's mother, was always set for dinner. Earlier a priest, presumably from across the street, said mass in a special shrine to St. Anthony in the garden where, according to Howard Johns in *Palm Springs Confidential*, Liberace worshipped every day.

Liberace's mother, Frances Zuchowski, who lived next door, always denied her son's homosexuality—at least to the public. (After her death, Liberace became friends with the new owners of her house and had a door cut through the wall that separated the houses so they could visit back and forth without attracting attention.) But Frances did convince Lee to buy a house for his (later estranged) brother George nearby in the hope that his proximity would help control Lee's outrageous behavior.

In addition to its gaudy furnishings, Liberace's Palm Springs house was filled with awards, among them six gold albums, commemorations for his two stars on Hollywood Boulevard, three "Pop Keyboard Artist of the Year" awards (1976–1979), and, of course, those two Emmys. In 1980 he was named both Star of the Year and Entertainer of the Year in Las Vegas, and he won the "Golden Mike" award in 1981 from the Pacific Pioneer Broadcasters. In 1982 he was voted to *Keyboard Magazine*'s Hall of Fame by its readers. But what really knocked the socks off millions of television viewers were not the awards—those he kept at home—but his showcase appearance on the Academy Awards broadcast that year performing the music from all five nominated films. (During the broadcast, his former lover Scott Thorson was forcibly removed from the penthouse of an apartment Liberace owned at 7461 Beverly Boulevard in Beverly Hills.)

Liberace considered one of his greatest achievements his founding in 1977, of the nonprofit Liberace Foundation for the Performing and Creative Arts, which funds scholarships for schools and colleges across the nation. Two years later he opened the Liberace Museum in Las Vegas, which serves as the money arm for the foundation.

He also wrote four books; besides the 1956 cookbook (which included "recipes from my seven dining rooms"), Liberace also wrote an autobiography, a book titled *The Things I Love*, and, in 1986 *The Wonderful Private World of Liberace*.

•••••

By the mid-1980s, Liberace was noticeably losing weight (he claimed he was on the then-popular "watermelon diet"). A chain smoker, he was suffering from advanced emphysema, heart disease, and, as it turned out, AIDS. After combining a tour promoting his final book with a two-week engagement at Radio City Music Hall in October 1986, he returned to Palm Springs. When his sister, Angelina Farrell, heard the rumors that Lee was very sick, she demanded that he be taken immediately to the Eisenhower Medical Center in Rancho Mirage. Word of Liberace's hospitalization leaked to the press, along with the news that his doctors had put him in quarantine, which at the time basically confirmed an AIDS diagnosis. After three days in the hospital, in January 1987 he went home to die.

For days, the media and hundreds of fans kept vigil outside the house while Lee cuddled his dogs (then numbering twenty-seven) and watched his favorite television show, *The Golden Girls*. At 2:05 P.M. on February 4, 1987, attended by Angelina, his sister-in-law Dora Liberace, and Jamie Wyatt, who was described as Liberace's "friend and long-time companion," he died. He was sixty-seven years old.

To prevent photography of the body when it was removed from the house, a special tent was erected for the coroner's van.

But that wasn't the end of it. The original cause of death was listed as "cardiac arrest due to cardiac failure, due to subacute encephalopathy, a contributing condition was aplastic anemia." Somehow that didn't ring right with the Riverside County coroner's office—apparently someone didn't want to list AIDS as the cause of death. So, despite the fact that Liberace's body had already been delivered to Forest Lawn Cemetery in the San Fernando Valley 100 miles away, it was shipped back for a post-embalming autopsy. After the autopsy (which among other things stated that he was nearly bald and had recently had a manicure), he was shipped back to Los Angeles and buried on February 7, wearing a wig, a white tuxedo, and of course full makeup. In his casket with him are a photo of Wyatt and one of his favorite dog, Wrinkles.

# CHAPTER TEN

## JANET AND CHARLIE

Today even the most innocent film fans probably know that a good number of their favorite stars in the middle of the twentieth century, despite the publicity of the era, were gay, lesbian, or bisexual.

As we have seen, however, even an obviously gay star such as Liberace ("obviously" to us now, though audiences of the time thought of his over-the-top effeminacy as just good fun) not only denied that he was gay, he even sued a British newspaper for implying that he was, and, as we saw previously, he won. So it's not surprising that the sexual identities of many other stars who lived in Palm Springs, before and long after Liberace's carryings-on, were not a subject for discussion in polite society, especially if they also enjoyed a high profile within the straight establishment, which basically ran the place until the 1980s or thereabouts.

That is why gossip rarely touched the reputations of Mary Martin, Janet Gaynor, and Charles Farrell, all of whom called

Palm Springs home for decades. It's particularly weird in the case of Martin and Gaynor, who, despite a number of marriages, were considered lovers by the Hollywood establishment for some three decades. Perhaps it's not such a long reach to suggest that it was because of a homophobic attitude on the part of the city's establishment of the era, that the pair would frequently escape to Europe together or, more significantly, spend months at a time—albeit with their husbands—at adjoining ranches in Brazil.

Charlie Farrell, after cofounding and running the raucous-for-years Racquet Club with fellow actor Ralph Bellamy and carving out a high-profile television career, would serve as the city's mayor from 1953 until 1960 and reign as its elder statesman until he died in 1990. Maybe his reputation is not so unusual since at the time of Farrell's greatest fame (and mayordom) the city began seeing conflict between the older, straight establishment types and an evolving gay majority. Furthermore Farrell was married to the silent film actress Virginia Valli from 1931 until her death in 1968, so how could he be gay? Go ask Gaynor, married at least once to a gay man; or Valentino's wife Natacha Rambova, or…well the list could go on and on, as we have seen.

•••••

In any film historian's book, Janet Gaynor ranks near the top. For one thing, she won the first Best Actress Oscar and, until Marlee Matlin won the Best Actress Oscar in 1986, was, at twenty-two, the youngest ever to win the award.

It was 1929, and playing catch-up in their first awards ceremony, the newly formed Academy of Motion Picture Arts and Sciences gave the petite Gaynor the award for three of her earlier films: *Sunrise*, *Seventh Heaven*, and *Street Angel* (the only time the Best Actress award was given for multiple performances).

In the latter pair of films her co-star was Charles Farrell, who would make eleven movies with Gaynor. They were known as "America's favorite lovebirds"; despite its age, director Frank Borzage's *Seventh Heaven*, the saga of a prostitute's love for a sewage worker (Farrell) through the trials of poverty, war, and death, still can bring tears. After his film career ended, Farrell would go on to television immortality of sorts starring as Gale Storm's dad Vern Albright in the sitcom *My Little Margie*.

Gaynor's first husband was an attorney named Jesse Lydell Peck whom she married in that halcyon year of 1929 (at least for her—victims of the Great Depression clearly thought differently) the couple divorced in 1933. She married her next husband, Gilbert Adrian, in 1939, and the union lasted until his death twenty years later. In 1964 Janet married producer Paul Gregory, a partnership that continued for another two decades until Gaynor's own death at seventy-seven in 1984.

The most famous of these marriages—and one of the most famous unions in Hollywood at the time—was undoubtedly that with Gilbert Adrian. Adrian (who used only his last name professionally) was for nearly three decades Hollywood's most famous costume designer. His creations brought style to 233 films, most of them for MGM, where, by improvising on a style started by fashion designer Elsa Schiaparelli in the early 1930s (by, among other details, padding the shoulders of women's clothes and lengthening the waists, which made the wearer seem more "in charge"), he created the still-famous, signature "looks" for Marlene Dietrich, Jean Harlow, Joan Crawford, and, most famously, Greta Garbo.

In the course of designing the costumes for 1939's *The Wizard of Oz*, Adrian would gain film immortality by having red sequins sewn onto a piece of pink chiffon which in turn was hand sewn onto a pair of patent leather shoes, thus creating Judy Garland's famous red slippers.

In 1940 the couple had a son, Robin Gaynor Adrian; unkind rumor has it that during labor, doctors told Adrian his wife might lose the baby, to which he replied, "Oh no, I'll have to go through that again!" According to C. David Heymann's authoritative biography *Liz*, Adrian was busy himself, being involved in a long affair with Elizabeth Taylor's father, Francis, while married to Gaynor. Not that Gaynor minded. In William Mann's meticulously researched book *Behind the Screen: How Gays and Lesbians Shaped Hollywood 1910-1969*, he says that Gaynor was a lifelong lesbian, seriously involved with at least two other stars: Margaret Livingston, a film vamp of the silent era who successfully segued into sound movies (she was the mistress of the legendary silent film producer Thomas Ince, and the wife of bandleader Paul Whiteman for nearly four decades) and, most famously, Mary Martin.

Janet Gaynor was born Laura Augusta Gainor on October 6, 1906, in Philadelphia, but she was raised in San Francisco, where her family moved when she was still a child. The reason has never been completely explained but, since the move came almost immediately after she was molested by her piano teacher, that event surely played a major role in the family's decision to relocate.

After graduating from high school in 1923, Gaynor decided to pursue a career in acting and, like thousands before her, moved to Los Angeles, where she paid the bills by working in a shoe store for $18 per week and picking up small, unbilled parts in a few features and comedy shorts. Then in 1926, when she was twenty, Gaynor managed to do what most Hollywood hopefuls of the era (and today) never accomplish—she was cast as the lead in a film. *The Johnstown Flood* was a melodrama about the 1889 Pennsylvania disaster; besides Gaynor's appearance, the film is also remembered for uncredited appearances of Carole Lombard (who played one of Gaynor's friends) and the twenty-five-year-old Clark Gable (seen in a group of men standing by a bar), who would soon return to the New York stage for five

years. In 1931 Gable was offered a contract by MGM and returned to Hollywood, where he soon made his first talkie, *The
Painted Desert*. Eleven more films followed that year including
*Susan Lennox (Her Fall and Rise)* starring Greta Garbo, and one
of Hollywood's greatest careers was finally launched.

Gaynor's performance in *The Johnstown Flood* showed Hollywood that the five-foot, curly-haired Gaynor had "star power,"
which in the silent-film era meant having a strong enough personality to bridge the technology gap between the screen and the
audience. Since silent-film story lines were inevitably driven by
pantomime, Charlie Chaplin, a master at telling a story through
body movements, gestures, and facial expressions, became the
era's greatest star. Gaynor also more than held her own against
co-star George O'Brien in 1927's *Sunrise*, one of the greatest
silent movies, despite the gay director F. W. Murnau's obvious
focus on O'Brien (a co-star was the previously mentioned Margaret Livingston).

Despite her rather high-pitched voice, Gaynor was one of
the silent stars who in 1928 was able to make a successful transi-
tion to sound, appearing memorably in the first version of *State
Fair* (1933) with Will Rogers and 1936's *Small Town Girl* with
James Stewart and Robert Taylor. In 1937 she would make the
film for which she is most famously remembered, playing Vicki
Lester in the first version of *A Star Is Born*, for which she was
nominated for a second Best Actress Oscar. (The film contained
several inside jokes, among them Gaynor's imitations of Katha-
rine Hepburn and Greta Garbo.) After making *Young at Heart*
a year later (it co-starred Douglas Fairbanks Jr.; she later said
that meeting his famous father was the high point of her 1929
Oscar awards evening), Gaynor, thirty-one, retired from movies. The reason was said to be the eclipsing of her star power at
Twentieth Century Fox by such rising talents as Loretta Young
and the mini-powerhouse Shirley Temple (Gaynor appeared in

1934's *Carolina* with the six-year-old Temple). Gaynor returned to films only once, in 1957, for a guest appearance in the saccharine Pat Boone film *Bernardine*.

When Adrian retired in 1953, the couple bought a 1,200 acre ranch 50 miles from Brasilia, the new capital of Brazil, and named it Nossa Faenza (our farm), where they raised coffee, chickens, and sugar. According to some accounts, this was also a way to get away from prying eyes that might note to her closeness to Mary Martin, who, with her husband, bought a farm next door to Gaynor and Adrian's. In any event, they remained there and both of them devoted themselves to painting, until Adrian returned to California in 1958 to design the costumes for the musical *Camelot* and a musical version of *Grand Hotel*. During the preliminary stages of this project, Adrian died suddenly at the age of fifty-six (his credit for the *Camelot* costume designs was posthumously shared with Tony Duquette); his death was later ruled a suicide. After his death, Gaynor continued painting and was honored with a showing of her still lifes in a New York gallery in 1976.

After Adrian's death Gaynor married Paul Gregory, and for much of the rest of their lives the pair lived at their Singing Tree Ranch in Desert Hot Springs, a few miles north of Palm Springs.

•••••

In September 1982 Gaynor's life and those of her husband, along with Mary Martin and Martin's friend and manager Ben Washer were forever tragically changed. As they were on their way to dinner in Janet's old hometown, San Francisco, a drunken driver named Robert Cato ran a red light and crashed broadside into their taxi at the corner of Franklin and California streets. The violent impact killed Washer instantly, and Gregory and Martin were seriously injured, with bruised organs and a few broken bones. Gaynor's injuries were thought for some time to be fatal: eleven broken ribs (the human body has only twelve!), a broken collarbone, a burst spleen, a ruptured bladder, a bleeding kidney, multiple pelvic fractures, and on top of all of that, her feet were mangled. Within minutes they were rushed to the trauma center at San Francisco General Hospital, where Janet was listed in critical condition with little hope of survival for more than a few days. During that night's five-hour surgery, she needed ten pints of blood.

That was just the beginning. Gaynor remained in the hospital for the next four months, during which she was operated on six more times. Then in January 1983 she went home to the Singing Tree Ranch to recover. She really never did, and the next eighteen months were a roller-coaster ride of setbacks and recovery. Finally, on September 14, 1984, Janet Gaynor died of pneumonia, renal failure, and other complications, all due to the accident.

She was interred in the Hollywood Forever Cemetery in Hollywood next to her second husband Adrian, but her stone reads "Janet Gaynor Gregory" in acknowledgment of her third husband.

"Most people stress the unhappiness in their careers," Gaynor once said. "I had a glorious twelve years in mine, as strange as it seems."

•••••

Can it be that some once famous people simply live long? So long that the legends about their lives and careers often overpower their actual personas—as in: "Greta Garbo was gay? You gotta be kidding!"

Actor Charles Farrell rose to fame in the silent-film era, easily segued into sound in 1929, became a television star in the

1950s after moving to Palm Springs, and, with fellow actor Ralph Bellamy, founded the resort that became the "in" place for a generation of Hollywood stars to escape. Then in 1953 he became mayor of the village for seven years, and afterward he faded into an elegant retirement as a sort of eminence of the town's establishment elite, dying at the age of eighty-nine.

Even today many residents of Palm Springs, some too young to have ever known him when he was mayor, angrily deny the possibility that he might have been gay (being married for thirty-seven years doesn't necessarily prove anything, as students of Hollywood history know well). "You're crazy" an acquaintance literally shouted at me when I broached the possibility.

The defenders of Farrell-as-a-straight-legend may be right, but probably not. Consider: we've seen that a young local named Paul Krueger claimed that he had slept with Farrell but, well, caution whispers, he was possibly a hustler. In *The Secret Life of Humphery Bogart*, author Darwin Porter says of Farrell, co-star with Bogart in 1931's *Body and Soul*: "Farrell, the future mayor of Palm Springs, was one of the screen's great lovers, most often romantically teamed with the perky and petite Janet Gaynor. The ironic joke on the American movie-going public was that both Farrell and Gaynor were gay." And author William Mann, in *Wisecracker*, his biography of William Haines (Chapter 13): "Charles Farrell, a gay actor who succeeded Billy (Haines) as number one at the box office … like his popular co-star Janet Gaynor, took solace in a happy marriage of convenience with Virginia Valli. Anita Page recalls dating Farrell around 1930 but giving him the heave-ho when she tired of the fact that he wore more makeup off screen than she did."

Not a lot of proof by any means, and the page quote might have been a clichéd response to being jilted by Farrell (Page, a leading lady in the early 1930s was romantically linked with Clark Gable and received several marriage proposals in the mail from, of all people, Benito Mussolini). Because Farrell, like Gaynor, had a fairly high-pitched voice—so, for that matter did John Gilbert, co-star and lover of Greta Garbo for a time, a voice that presumably ended his career when sound arrived— and had a noticeably effeminate manner, "some," according to Anthony Slide in his book *Silent Topics: Essays on Undocumented Areas of Silent Films*, "assumed he was gay. Any marriage Farrell entered into would be one of convenience with the implication that his wife, actress Virginia Valli, was a lesbian. Yet there is no evidence to support such a conclusion." Or at least there was no evidence Slide and many others wanted to notice. Nevertheless, because of Farrell's perceived effeminacy, director Mark Sandrich cast him in his otherwise heavy-handed 1933 comedy *Aggie Appleby, Maker of Men* as a prissy socialite who is "butched-up" by Wynne Gibson (playing Aggie) to be a construction gang boss before being rescued by his old fiancée played by the pre-Westinghouse spokesperson Betty Furness.

•••••

Born in Walpole, Massachusetts, on August 9, 1901, Farrell studied for a business career at Boston University before deciding to switch professional gears by coming to Hollywood and breaking into films as an extra. Like Gaynor, he succeeded, a nearly impossible challenge at the time when the Hollywood Chamber of Commerce estimated only one in 20,000 would succeed, numbers that led directly to the casting couch as a means to improve the odds. Yet, probably because Farrell was extremely handsome, tall (6 feet, 2 inches), athletic, and possessing a graceful elegance combined with an all-American, clean-cut sex appeal—exactly like Billy Haines—he did it. After a brief apprenticeship in Mack Sennett's two-reelers, Farrell began his rise to stardom at Fox Studios.

His first film appearance was in an uncredited bit part in 1923's *The Cheat*, which starred the Polish-born screen vamp Pola Negri who later claimed to be Rudolph Valentino's last lover and who made a notorious scene at his 1926 funeral when she threw herself on his casket. Farrell's second film role was another uncredited part in the enormously popular 1923 film adaptation of the Victor Hugo novel *The Hunchback of Notre Dame*, starring Lon Chaney. Then he broke out in 1926's *Old Ironsides*, during which an explosion damaged his hearing, an infirmity Farrell tried to hide for the rest of his life.

Gaynor and Farrell were first paired in the 1927 romantic classic *Seventh Heaven* and then in the similarly themed redemption film *Street Angel*. Their last silent film together was *Lucky Star* (1929), in which Charles played Tim, a good man struggling with life in a wheelchair after being wounded in World War I. His performance was poignant and unforgettable.

The popularity of the Gaynor/Farrell team survived the switch-over to talkies, especially when both Gaynor and Farrell proved to have pleasant singing voices in 1929's *Sunny Side Up*. Farrell's odd New England accent led many to believe he was British, an assumption that he did little to discourage. As the 1930s progressed, Farrell's stardom diminished, and by 1938 he, like Gaynor, was playing second fiddle to their studio's newest attraction, Shirley Temple.

In 1931 Farrell and actor Ralph Bellamy opened the Racquet Club in Palm Springs after being thrown off the tennis court at the El Mirador resort when Marlene Dietrich wanted to play. Their place was an instant hit with the stars, who wanted to get away from the pressures of the film capital—or hide out from them. As an example of the bonhomie that Bellamy and Farrell brought to the place, they charged for Coca-Cola at the famous Bamboo Bar, but the beer was free. (At least one entrepreneur tried unsuccessfully to reopen the place as an all gay resort in recent years, and now it is a condominium development.)

In 1953, a year after he was cast to co-star with Gale Storm in *My Little Margie*, Farrell was elected mayor of Palm Springs. After *Margie*'s run ended in 1955, he headlined 1956's *Charles Farrell Show*, a sitcom that was virtually a thirty-nine-week commercial for both Palm Springs and his Racquet Club.

Was he gay? I guess that's for you to draw your own conclusion.

Oh yes: while I was writing this chapter, a Palm Springs friend called and said, "You know something? I mentioned your conviction that Charlie Farrell was gay to a person who was a friend of his. She said, 'Of course he was gay. Everyone knew it.'"

# CHAPTER ELEVEN

# MARY

While Janet Gaynor was painting at her ranch in Brazil, next door Mary Martin was—at least until her husband Richard Halliday died in 1973 and she returned to theater work—doing her needlepoint. It was all very domestic, and hardly what one would expect when one considers either actor's career, especially Martin's.

Who, of a certain generation, can forget Mary Martin's exuberant rendition of "I'm Gonna Wash that Man Right Outta My Hair" from Rodgers and Hammerstein's hit musical *South Pacific*, in which she originated the role of Nellie Forbush on Broadway in 1949?

When it came to her personal life, however, despite two marriages, she didn't have much of a problem with washing men out of her hair—they never got that close. There is evidence that convinces many that for thirty years or so she and the legendary film star Janet Gaynor (Chapter 10), were lovers.

A decade after *South Pacific*, Martin created the role of Maria

Von Trapp in the Broadway production of Rodgers and Hammerstein's *The Sound of Music*, for which she was nearly as famous.

But for an entire generation, long before Sandy Duncan and Cathy Rigby, Mary Martin *was* Peter Pan. Her association with the character began with a Jerome Robbins–produced Broadway version of the story in 1954, co-starring Cyril Richard as Captain Hook, with music by Jule Styne and lyrics by Betty Comden and Adolph Green. But what really made people across America indelibly identify her with J. M. Barrie's elfinlike boy who loved to fly and refused to grow up were three television broadcasts of the musical that year and the next as well as a taped version broadcast in 1960 and several times thereafter.

In her autobiography, *My Heart Belongs* (acknowledging her first hit record, "My Heart Belongs to Daddy" by Cole Porter), Martin wrote: "Peter Pan is perhaps the most important thing, to me, that I have ever done in the theater. I cannot even remember a day when I didn't want to be Peter. When I was a child I was sure I could fly. In my dreams I often did, and it was always the same: I ran, raised my arms like a great bird, soared into the sky, flew.

"I wish I could express in words the joy I felt in flying," Mary Martin wrote about the experience of soaring above the stage (supported by wires), every night in the show. "I loved it so. The freedom of spirit—the thing Peter always felt—was suddenly there for me. I discovered I was happier in the air than on the ground."

And of course, it is that seemingly endless human search for such freedom of spirit that has made the character of Peter Pan and, for years, its personification by Martin, so iconic in the lives of millions of homosexual men and women.

•••••

Mary Virginia Martin was born in Weatherford, Texas, on

December 11, 1913, the second daughter of a local lawyer and his wife, a violin teacher who began teaching Mary how to play the instrument at an early age. But Mary showed more enthusiasm for singing and dancing, so when she was twelve, she began taking voice lessons. At an early age she began singing as one of three little girls who performed on Saturday nights at a bandstand just outside the courtroom where her father worked. "Even in those days without microphones," she has recalled, "my high piping voice carried all over the square. I have always thought that I inherited my carrying voice from my father."

In 1930, when Martin was sixteen, her parents sent her to the prestigious Ward Belmont finishing school in Nashville, Tennessee, but she left after two months to marry her boyfriend, twenty-one-year-old Benjamin Jackson Hagman, an accountant. The couple returned to Weatherford, where they lived with her parents; Hagman then studied to become a lawyer and later worked in his father-in-law's office. On September 21, 1931, the seventeen-year-old Martin gave birth to Lawrence Martin Hagman, who, under the name Larry Hagman, would become a well-known television actor, starring from 1965 until 1970 in the situation comedy *I Dream of Jeannie* and for nearly a decade and a half after 1978 as the ruthless J. R. Ewing on the prime-time soap opera *Dallas*.

Martin, says of these times: "I was seventeen, a married woman without real responsibilities, miserable about my mixed-up emotions, afraid there was something awfully wrong with me because I didn't enjoy being a wife. Worst of all, I didn't have enough to do." What she decided to do was to open a dancing school (she had originally been taught by her older teacher and by watching dancers in movies), and basically left the raising of her son to her mother.

Her school was such a success that, after a season, Martin went to Hollywood and enrolled at the Fanchon and Marco

School of Theater to improve her dancing skills. (Fanchon and Marco were a brother and sister dancing team that not only taught dancing but fielded a troupe similar to New York City's Rockettes that appeared at the Paramount Theater in Hollywood and several other cities.) For the next few years she alternated between teaching dance in Texas and studying in Hollywood where she was able to pick up a few singing engagements, at least enough to convince her to move permanently to the film capital in 1936; there she hoped to make a living as a performer. She and Hagman were divorced in 1937 (according to one source, Hagman claimed Mary had been having an affair with his ex-wife); she was given custody of Larry but placed him in a series of private schools and military academies so she would be free to pursue her career.

Martin, who continued to teach dance, gradually found nightclub work at, among several gigs, the still-famous Cine-grille in the Hollywood Roosevelt Hotel, where she earned some $400 a week—a huge amount at the time and the equivalent of some $5,000 weekly today. Like every young show business hopeful in the film capital, she constantly auditioned for film and theater work; unlike most, she soon got work acting in bit parts and dubbing the singing voices of others (among them Gypsy Rose Lee's voice in 1938's *Battle of Broadway*). That year she also got the break that was to shape her career: she was spotted by Broadway producer Laurence Schwab at a talent show at the famed Trocadero nightclub. Impressed by her singing and personality, he signed Martin for an upcoming Broadway musical. By the time she got to New York, however, the show had fallen through, so Martin auditioned for another upcoming show that had suffered a last-minute defection and was cast in the Cole Porter musical *Leave It to Me!* What followed was a real-life example of the show business fantasy of overnight success.

•••••

In *Leave It to Me!* Martin, although in a secondary role, created a sensation when the show opened in November 1938 singing the risque, "My Heart Belongs to Daddy," accompanied by a partial striptease. Later that month she recorded the song with Eddy Duchin and His Orchestra, and although record charts did not exist at the time, chart researcher Joel Whitburn estimates it was a Top Ten hit. Two weeks later she was on the cover of *Life* magazine; immediately after, she recorded of a series of singles with Woody Herman and His Orchestra. On January 11, 1939, two months after opening as an unknown on Broadway, Martin opened an eight-week nightclub engagement at the famous Rainbow Room atop Rockefeller Center, appearing each night after finishing her work in *Leave It to Me!*

Although she had spent two years vainly knocking on Hollywood's door, now that she was famous elsewhere, Paramount offered her a featured role in *The Great Victor Herbert.* But she didn't close other doors; before the movie's release in December 1939 she returned to New York, joined the cast of a radio show, and signed to star in a new Laurence Schwab musical *Nice Goin'.* The show closed out of town but, while in the East, she recorded her first album for Decca, *Mary Martin in an Album of Cole Porter Songs*, which included another rendition of "My Heart Belongs to Daddy."

On May 5, 1940, Martin married Richard Halliday, a Paramount story editor, and soon began making her second Paramount feature, co-starring in *Rhythm on the River* with Bing Crosby, the studio's biggest star. She then immediately segued into another film, *Love Thy Neighbor*, co-starring with radio superstars Jack Benny and Fred Allen. A film career was exploding as she went on to make several other films (including *Birth of the Blues,* again with Crosby) before giving birth to a daughter, Mary Heller Halliday, in November 1941.

Success continued to build on success. In January 1942, Martin became the regular female vocalist on Crosby's radio show the *Kraft Music Hall,* one of the biggest shows on what was then the world's most influential medium, and also continued her recording career. If Martin made any mistakes at this point in her career, it was flipping a coin to choose between two Broadway-bound shows that were offered to her in 1943: *Green Grow the Lilacs* by the newly formed duo of composer Richard Rodgers and lyricist Oscar Hammerstein, and *Dancing in the Streets* by lyricist Howard Dietz and tunesmith Vernon Duke (of *April in Paris* fame). The coin came up for *Dancing in the Streets,* which closed before reaching New York. *Green Grow the Lilacs* opened on Broadway on March 31, 1943, as *Oklahoma!*

Although another movie quickly followed—her ninth, *True to Life,* with Franchot Tone and Dick Powell—Martin had decided to focus on a stage career and moved back to New York. She was soon cast as the lead in *One Touch of Venus,* the story of a Greek statue that comes to life in current-day Manhattan, with a book by S. J. Perelman and Ogden Nash, lyrics by Nash, and music by Kurt Weill. For her performance, Martin won a Donaldson Award, the precursor to the Tony Award, and Decca lost no time recording the second-ever "original Broadway cast" album (the first was *Oklahoma!*). She also did her part for the war effort, recording a Top Ten rendition of the standard "I'll Walk Alone."

The day after the February 1945 close of *One Touch of Venus,* Martin and Halliday embarked on a national tour of the musical, during which they decided that Halliday should give up his work as a story editor and devote himself to being her manager. He filled that function for the rest of his life. After the tour, she was cast in a new musical, *Lute Song,* a love story based on a fourteenth-century Chinese play, which, although a critical success (including the song "Mountain High, Valley Low") lasted only a couple of months, as did her next effort, Noel Coward's *Pacific 1860*, which opened in London in December 1946.

One of the hit shows back home in America was Irving Berlin's musical *Annie Get Your Gun*, starring Ethel Merman. Since Merman wasn't interested in going on the road with the story of the Western sharpshooter, Martin was offered the job. She took it, toured with the show for nearly a year, and won a special Tony in 1948, the award's second year.

Lightning really struck when Martin opened on Broadway on April 7, 1949, in a show based on World War II stories by James Michener; *South Pacific* would be her greatest career triumph. She starred in it for two years (and in London for a third year), winning her second Tony, and the original cast album stayed at the top of the charts for sixty-nine weeks, selling several million copies (during the run she also recorded a duet single with her son Larry of "You're Just in Love" from Ethel Merman's current show, *Call Me Madam*). Columbia Records also contracted her to record a series of studio-cast versions of music from musicals that had run prior to the era of the original Broadway cast album (and the 1948 invention of the long-playing record). These included Cole Porter's *Anything Goes*, Rodgers and Hart's *Babes in Arms*, and George and Ira Gershwin's *Girl Crazy*, all recorded in 1950 and 1951. These were followed by her final appearance in a feature film, playing herself along with such theater stalwarts as Shirley Booth, Lionel and Ethel Barrymore, Talullah Bankhead, Richard Rodgers, Helen Hayes, and dozens of others, credited and uncredited, in *Main Street to Broadway*, a movie made primarily to promote Broadway theater.

By now Martin and her husband were convinced that the future demanded putting together their own projects. The first effort was certainly auspicious: a musical adaptation of *Peter Pan*, which opened on Broadway on October 20, 1954. The show ran only 152 performances—it was contractually forced to close so as not to compete with an upcoming live NBC television broadcast. Nevertheless, she won her third Tony Award for her performance, and the cast album became a hit. On March 7, only nine days after her final stage performance as the boy who loved flying, Mary Martin herself flew into theatrical immortality before a reported television audience of 65 million, winning an Emmy Award in the process.

Vacationing in South America after *Peter Pan*, Martin and Halliday decided to buy a farm in Anápolis, Brazil, and they lived there off and on for years when they weren't at their place in Rancho Mirage near Palm Springs or when Martin was working. Next door, Janet Gaynor and Adrian had a similar ranch, and it is said that the arrangement provided a very private means for Mary and Janet to be together far from Hollywood's (and Manhattan's) probing eyes.

•••••

But in the near future there was a lot of work to be done, including the two-performance-a-day grind of an eighty-seven-city concert tour. Even more involving was Richard and Mary's next project, for which they obtained the rights and were assembling the creative team: a musical adaptation of the memoirs of Austrian Maria von Trapp relating her wartime escape from the Nazis with her singing troupe, the Trapp Family Singers. It became, of course, *The Sound of Music*, with songs by Rodgers and Hammerstein; it opened on Broadway November 16, 1959, and Martin starred in it for two years of the show's three-and-a-half year run, won her fourth Tony, and recorded the cast album, which sold in the millions and brought her her first Grammy Award.

Because she was committed to the 1963 musical *Jennie*, which was based on the life of actress Laurette Taylor, a silent screen

star who made a famous comeback on the Broadway stage playing the Southern matriarch Amanda Wingfield in the original
1945 Broadway production of the Tennessee Williams play *The
Glass Menagerie*, Martin had to turn down the lead in *Hello, Dolly!*
which instead famously starred Carol Channing. But she was able
to do the national tour, which began in April 1965, crisscrossed
the United States for the next five months, and then in the Pacific
Theater (as it was called in WWII) before she opened the London
production. Martin made her final appearance in a Broadway musical in *I Do! I Do!* which ran for a year and a half on Broadway
followed by a thirty-city road tour, at the end of which she went
to Brazil determined to retire (she opened her own boutique in
Anápolis and also wrote a book on needlepoint).

After Richard Halliday died at sixty-seven in 1973, she sold
the farm in Brazil and moved back to the United States, living
on Martha's Vineyard and in Rancho Mirage. In 1978, Martin
was reportedly offered the role of Miss Ellie, in *Dallas*, which
she turned down (Barbara Bel Geddes took the part). Had she
accepted, a television audience of millions would have had the
unique opportunity of seeing a television mother and son played
by a real-life mother and son. (Hagman earlier had appeared in
the chorus of *South Pacific*).

She worked occasionally before and after the September 1982
car accident in San Francisco in which her friend and agent was
killed and which was nearly fatal to her beloved Janet Gaynor
(see Chapter 10); four years later she toured for all of 1986 in
James Kirkwood's comedy *Legends!* with Carol Channing.

It would be her last stage work. By December 1989, when
she was honored by the Kennedy Center, Martin was suffering
from the colon cancer that would end her life on November 3,
1990, at the age of seventy-six. The year before her death, Martin saw her 1960 performance in *Peter Pan* sell four million
videocassettes.

# CHAPTER TWELVE

## JAMES AND JOHN

In a community that was populated by so many stars in its heyday—both straight and gay—delicious stories are always lying just under the duvet of time, waiting to be discovered. And one of them is especially fascinating.

Is there a gay person who didn't see the 1998 film *Gods and Monsters*, if only to ogle the hunky Brendan Fraser in the near-buff? The film, which won the Best Adapted Screenplay Oscar, was based on Christopher Bram's 1995 novelized version of silent film director James Whale's last days, *The Father of Frankenstein*. It was recently described as a "fantasy" based on the life of the once famous (and notoriously gay for his time) director. In the film, Whale was portrayed by the incomparable (and gay) actor Sir Ian McKellan, who received a Best Actor nomination for his performance (Lynn Redgrave, who played Whale's housekeeper, was nominated for Best Supporting Actress).

But completely missing from contemporary memory of James Whale's life is the fact that from 1953 or thereabouts until May

1957, when he committed suicide by drowning himself in the pool of his home in the Los Angeles suburb of Pacific Palisades (later owned by Goldie Hawn), he owned an eight-unit hotel in Palm Springs. It was named the Town and Desert, boasted a 40-foot pool, and provided free bicycles for guests. But, as fans of *Gods and Monsters* remember, Whale, who indulged his passion for drawing and painting in the mornings, indulged his passion for men by filling his pool with nude young hunks in the afternoons while he, who had a mortal fear of water, fooled around in the shallow end or simply took in the fetching scenery.

So, considering Whale's proclivities, it's no stretch of the imagination at all to assume that he often filled his hotel's pool in Palm Springs with similarly nude, bronzed young men on weekends. James Whale's Town and Desert Hotel would therefore have been the first clothing-optional resort—by at least a generation—in Palm Springs.

As many have forgotten (or never known about) Whale's connection with Palm Springs, so too many have forgotten his tremendous contribution to film in both his native England and his adopted Hollywood. As the titles of both Bram's book and the film remind us, it was Whale's monsters that contributed to a significant part of his fame. And it was the black humor with which he treated his monsters, mixing giggles with shudders, that raised both films from typical horror films to lasting film art as similar efforts fell by Hollywood's wayside. His unique point of view is certainly there in *Frankenstein* (1931), but even more so in 1935's *The Bride of Frankenstein*, both also paving the way for such cult hits as *The Rocky Horror Picture Show* (1975), television's *The Munsters*, and such riffs on Whale's own work as Mel Brooks' 1974 film *Young Frankenstein*.

In making these and his other films, Whale also provided a link to a large underground network of gay and lesbian talent including the great Charles Laughton, whom Whale cast first in a movie in England in 1924 and then in his 1932 Universal film *The Old Dark House*, the actor's American film debut. (Its plot, involving a group of stranded travelers who take refuge in an amusingly strange but sinister house, has been the pattern for several films, including, certainly, *The Rocky Horror Picture Show*.) Other Brits whose careers he fostered were Laughton's actress wife Elsa Lanchester (Frankenstein's bride with the memorably frizzy hair), and Colin Clive, who played Frankenstein (remember, Frankenstein was the *doctor* who created the monster, played memorably by Boris Karloff in both films). Clive, who died at thirty-seven of acute alcoholism—that's what forced "Hollywood" marriages occasionally did to gay actors—was said to have been cast because Whale had a crush on him.

As a rather delicious footnote to all this, the career of the actress Gloria Stuart, ninety-eight at this writing, was launched when Whale cast her in *The Old Dark House*, and in the following year's *The Invisible Man* (*The Invisible Man* was an impressive early use of special effects when the bandages that covered the invisible man's face—hitherto one only heard the voice of Claude Rains—were unwrapped to reveal: nothing). Despite her success as an elegant blonde leading lady in many 1930s films (in 1933 alone Stuart made nine films), her career petered out in the mid-1940s and, aside from a few small jobs, she was largely forgotten. Then in 1997 James Cameron cast her as the elderly version of Kate Winslet's character in *Titanic*, which brought her a Best Supporting Actress Oscar nomination. Stuart, then eighty-seven, who began her career sixty-five years earlier, said the honor had been worth the wait.

There is another side to this history that is also rooted in the gay subculture. Since the publication of Mary Shelley's book in 1818, Frankenstein has been regarded rather simplistically by some critics as a homoerotic fantasy of a man determined to produce children without recourse to a woman (despite countless examples of gay men managing to do it). It is further argued that this was the reason why Whale, upon his arrival in America, promptly chose the Frankenstein project as his first film.

It is far more likely that the project provided Whale with another opportunity to work with Colin Clive, whom, as was noted, he was probably involved with romantically and may have been having a relationship with four years earlier when he cast Clive to replace the twenty-one-year-old Laurence Olivier in a London production of R. C. Sherriff's antiwar play *Journey's End*. It has been suggested that Whale was most likely attracted to the Frankenstein story because it was about an intelligent and talented man who makes bad decisions and thus dooms himself to a miserable fate. It is a theme that Whale would return to in films and that would define his own life as well, as is clearly detailed in both *Gods and Monsters* and Bram's book.

Boris Karloff was cast as the monster after Whale and Bela Lugosi, celebrated as 1931's *Dracula*, couldn't agree on the approach to the monster's character. Lugosi apparently wanted to play the part closer to Mary Shelley's original monster, who had dialogue; as filmed by Whale, there were no lines for the character to speak.

Karloff, whose real name was William Henry Pratt (he apparently picked his stage name out of the air), had just about everything going against his becoming a film star before he was chosen by Whale. He was bow-legged, had a stutter as well as a lisp, certainly didn't possess matinee idol looks, and earned a living between film gigs by both working as a day laborer and selling ice cream. In one of those pre-"Frankenstein" roles, that of a murderous convict in 1931's *The Criminal Code*, his size was used to create an atmosphere of fear, which the actor then softened by playing the character as a child longing for his father's love, a concept that led directly to *Frankenstein*'s monster.

What Karloff clearly did to overcome his disabilities as well as secure a niche in the Hollywood pantheon was to follow Lon Chaney's advice: "The secret of success in Hollywood lies in being different from anyone else. Find something no one else can or will do—and they'll begin to take notice of you. Hollywood is full of competent actors. What the screen needs is individuality."

Clearly, much the same could also be said for much of the career of James Whale.

•••••

James Whale was born July 22, 1889, in Dudley, England, the sixth of the seven children of a blast furnace operator and a nurse. He was considered too weak to follow his brothers into the local heavy industries, so he started working as a cobbler. Before long he discovered a talent for sign writing and used the additional income to pay for evening classes at the Dudley School of Arts and Crafts.

In October 1915, after making a living as a newspaper cartoonist for a couple years, Whale enlisted in the army and was commissioned as a second lieutenant. He was taken a prisoner by the Germans in August 1917 and, while imprisoned, not only managed to continue his love of drawing but also discovered a talent for staging theatrical productions.

After the armistice he embarked on a professional stage career. In 1928 he was offered the opportunity to direct two performances of *Journey's End.* It was a huge success and moved to the West End with the twenty-eight-year-old Colin Clive replacing, as noted, the original lead, Laurence Olivier, and then it ran for 600 performances. Its success brought Whale to America, where he directed the Broadway stage version in 1930, and then to Hollywood, where Whale made his film directing debut with the film adaptation of the play, with Clive cast in the lead.

Remembered best for the black humor he displayed in *Fran-*

*kenstein* and *The Bride of Frankenstein,* Whale was also one of the first directors to move the camera fluidly through the shot. The films of F. W. Murnau, have been mentioned as a major influence on Whale's moving camera technique. Murnau, whose most famous film was 1922's *Nosferatu* (an adaptation of Bram Stoker's *Dracula*) was famously gay and a close friend of Greta Garbo. He died in 1931 after an accident on the highway between Los Angeles and Santa Barbara, when the car, driven by a fourteen-year-old hustler, went off the road into a ditch. Murnau was reportedly performing fellatio on him at the time.

Film historians assert that Universal Pictures owed its success in the 1930s in large part to the box-office receipts from Whale's three blockbusters (the two *Frankenstein* films and *The Invisible Man*). His pictures also made the careers of Gloria Stuart, Colin Clive, Elsa Lanchester, Boris Karloff, and Claude Rains, to name just a few, most of whom Whale knew in England. Whale was also responsible for such major films as the original *Waterloo Bridge* (1931), and 1936's *Show Boat,* starring Irene Dunne and the legendary bass Paul Robeson as Joe. Robeson's communist leanings would a decade later make him highly controversial and essentially unemployable.

Whale intended to crown his career with 1937's *The Road Back,* based on Erich Maria Remarque's sequel to *All Quiet on the Western Front.* It didn't turn out that way, however; the film was a major flop—but its failure had little to do with Whale's work. As *Gods and Monsters* moviegoers may remember, Whale, as played by McKellen, claims to have hated making the movie, but his anger was more about what happened to the film after he finished it. Worried that the director's portrayal of the contemporary Nazi regime as warmongers (Germany was a major source of foreign film revenue), Universal recut the movie over Whale's angry protest to appease the German government.

In 1937 Whale also made *The Great Garrick*, a fictional comedy about the eighteenth-century actor and playwright David Garrick (for Warner Brothers); despite its starring Brian Aherne and Olivia de Havilland (and Lana Turner in a small part), it was another flop, as was *Port of Seven Seas*, his only MGM film, adapted from Marcel Pagnol's *Fanny* trilogy. *Wives Under Suspicion*, his next to last film at Universal, was an unsuccessful remake of his 1933 film *The Kiss Before the Mirror*. *The Man in the Iron Mask* in 1939, starring Louis Hayward and Joan Bennett, was Whale's last big success; afterward he made *Green Hell* for Universal, an ordinary jungle adventure starring Douglas Fairbanks Jr., Joan Bennett, and Vincent Price; it was his last full-length film. In the 1940s he made a featurette, an adaptation of a one-act play by William Saroyan, which was never released; he never made another film.

In 1929 Whale and David Lewis, a young story editor and later a producer, began a relationship that would last nearly three decades. The sexual component of their relationship—an open secret in Hollywood at the time—was said to have ended in the early 1950s, but they remained friends until Whale's death. After a series of strokes left Whale physically depleted, emotionally unstable, prone to memory difficulties, lonely and suffering from depression—all of which were touched on in the film—Whale drowned himself. But it would be thirty years before the public learned that his death was a suicide and not a terrible accident as it was portrayed at the time. In 1987, shortly before his own death, Lewis made public Whale's suicide note. It read: "The future is just old age and illness and pain...I must have peace and this is the only way."

Hollywood never officially ostracized Whale (there were too many gay players for that to happen), but his flamboyant lifestyle was said to be frowned-upon by such famous members of Hollywood's elite as the gay director George Cukor, whose celebrity-packed party is one of the set pieces in *Gods and Monsters*.

•••••

Undoubtedly some of those nude young men that filled Whale's swimming pools in Pacific Palisades and probably in Palm Springs were hustlers. And perhaps some of them were as seemingly naive as Joe Buck in 1969's film *Midnight Cowboy* although Buck—played by a relatively unknown, thirty-year-old Jon Voight—came to New York to sell himself to women, not men. Nevertheless, in the film there is a clear homosexual subtext, which its gay director, John Schlesinger (who was still closeted), treats like a hot stove, both in the portrayal of Buck's frantic attempt to make money by sleeping with a man and in his relationship with a third-rate con man, Ratso Rizzo, played by Dustin Hoffman.

Schlesinger won the Best Director Oscar, one of *Midnight Cowboy*'s three Academy Awards of its seven nominations; the other Oscars were for Best Picture and Best Screenplay from Another Medium. It's an impressive achievement for the Britisher's first U.S. film and the first—and only—X-rated film to win the award. Both Voight and Hoffman were also nominated for their performances but lost the Best Actor statuette to John Wayne for his performance in *True Grit*.

Despite soft-pedaling Joe Buck's homosexual activity in *Midnight Cowboy* (it was far more explicit in John Herlihy's 1965 novel, but there were lines even an X-rated film couldn't cross in 1969), homosexual themes in fact permeated many of the films Schlesinger made before and after *Midnight Cowboy*.

During a BBC interview in 1993, Schlesinger claimed that,

starting with his 1965 breakthrough, *Darling* (which won three Oscars, including the Best Actress award for Julie Christie, whom Schlesinger had first cast in her breakout film, 1963's *Billy Liar*), he made it a point to include gay characters in his movies. This was certainly the case with 1971's *Sunday Bloody Sunday*, a drama—which Schlesinger said was semibiographical—about a sculptor (played by Murray Head) torn between a divorced woman (Glenda Jackson) and a male lawyer (Peter Finch). In the interview Schlesinger recalled heated discussions with his screenwriter, Penelope Gilliatt, over the scene in which Head's character greeted Finch's with a kiss. "There was a sort of fashion for doing everything—don't let's get too involved, let's remove it from us," Gilliatt argued. To which Schlesinger replied: "No, it's got to be done absolutely as if it's an everyday occurrence with everything totally natural and normal about it. If we had done it any other way it wouldn't have worked.

"I think this was a breakthrough film," Schlesinger later wrote of *Sunday Bloody Sunday*, "where gay characters were not tortured, suicidal, mean, bitchy, dishonorable, or tragic—they were portrayed as normal, loving human beings with real lives, real careers, [and] real feelings filled with compassion." The director regarded the story as a personal statement and his own coming out publicly as gay.

In the 1970s, Schlesinger went on to direct Dustin Hoffman again as a runner terrorized by a Nazi dentist (Laurence Olivier) in *Marathon Man*, and Richard Gere as a U.S. soldier stationed in World War II England in *Yanks*. He also helmed 1975's less-than-successful screen adaptation of Nathanael West's iconic novel of Hollywood in the 1930s, *The Day of the Locust*.

Latter-day credits included: 1985's *The Falcon and the Snowman*, 1988's *Madame Sousatzka* with Shirley MacLaine as an eccentric music teacher, and 1990's *Pacific Heights*, which critic Roger Ebert called "a horror film for yuppies."

John Schlesinger was born February 16, 1926, in London, one of three children of a physician and his wife. From childhood he was fascinated by cameras, and he began making films when still a child, using an amateur movie camera. After graduating from Uppingham school (also attended by Hugh Jackman, Boris Karloff, and the actor Stephen Fry [*Wilde*, *Gosford Park*], who was expelled from Uppingham when he was fifteen), he joined the army on his eighteenth birthday in 1944. Although Schlesinger expected to receive a commission in the Royal Engineers, he ended up in an entertainment unit performing widely as a magician after it was discovered that he suffered from vertigo (and also caught rheumatic fever and broke his leg) during engineer corps training.

Between 1947 and 1950 Schlesinger studied English literature at Balliol College, Oxford, where he also joined the dramatic society and, with a friend, made a pair of short films. Schlesinger then began a career as a small-part actor, starting in *The Alchemist* with the Oxford Players and touring with a number of plays. He made his film acting debut in 1952's *Singlehanded*, a war film that starred Jeffrey Hunter. In 1955 he played in *Mourning Becomes Electra*, directed by Peter Hall, and he acted in several episodes of the television series *Ivanhoe* and *Robin Hood*, where his director was Lindsay Anderson, later to become famous as the counter-culture director who won the Cannes Film Festival's grand prize for 1968's *If...*, a savage satire of English public school life.

For five years commencing in 1956 Schlesinger worked at the BBC directing documentaries and features, among which one was about the Cannes Film Festival; one was a portrait of Georges Simenon, the Belgian writer whose 350-book output included a hundred Inspector Maigret whodunits; one was about the famed British composer Benjamin Britten; another was about Italian opera; and one called *Private View* was a study of four young painters. For directing *Terminus*, a thirty-three-minute documentary about a day in the life of London's Waterloo (railroad)

Station (1961), he was honored with the Gold Lion award at the Venice film festival as well as the British Academy Award.

John Schlesinger's first feature film, *A Kind of Loving*, made in 1962 (it made a star of Alan Bates), won the Golden Bear at the Berlin Film Festival. This was seen as part of the New Wave realist movement in British cinema that included Tony Richardson, Karel Reisz, and Lindsay Anderson,

In 1970 he was appointed a Commander of the British Empire (CBE); nevertheless, other than for the huge success of 1976's *Marathon Man*, his theatrical and film efforts never returned to the previous success that had made him internationally famous. He also returned to television, where he took on another gay theme in the 1983 television play *The Englishman Abroad*, with Alan Bates as the flamboyantly gay spy Guy Burgess, and in 1991 he directed *A Question of Attribution*, a television play and companion piece to *The Englishman Abroad* but focusing on Burgess's fellow double agent Anthony Blunt.

In 1966 John Schlesinger began a lifelong relationship with the photographer Michael Childers, who gained fame for his portraits of many film icons.

In 2000 Schlesinger underwent a multiple heart bypass operation, followed by a stroke at the end of 2001 from which he never fully recovered. The following year, when he was awarded the lifetime achievement award by the British Academy of Film and Television Arts, his acceptance speech was read by Dustin Hoffman. In July 2003, he was admitted to the Desert Region Medical Center near his Palm Springs home, suffering breathing difficulties. On the 24th of that month, with Childers at his bedside, he was taken off life support and died.

John Schlesinger's memorial, at least among gay movie fans, is his courage not to portray homosexuals in film as caricatures (as many directors have done and continue to do), but to treat them with respect as human beings.

# CHAPTER THIRTEEN

# BILLY AND EDMUND

It's only a short drive from Palm Springs to the Rancho Mirage, site of one of the grandest estates in America. Appropriately named "Sunnylands" built by the late publisher Walter Annenberg, the 32,000-square-foot house is situated on 400 acres planted with rare cacti, boasts a nine-hole golf course, and has a guest book signed by such visitors as Queen Elizabeth II, her husband Prince Philip, her sister Princess Margaret, her children Prince Charles and Prince Andrew, and Presidents Eisenhower (who retired nearby), Nixon, Ford, Reagan, Bush (41), and Clinton, among dozens of others, including local Hollywood superstars Frank Sinatra and Bob Hope.

The place also played a part in a footnote in the life of the area as well as American history. It was at Sunnylands on December 6, 1968, that President-elect Richard Nixon, accompanied by the future president and nearby resident Gerald Ford (then Republican House of Representatives leader), and California governor Ronald Reagan, visited Sunnylands and offered Annenberg the most prestigious diplomatic appointment a president can make: the ambassadorship to Great Britain. "What impresses me most is his strong character," Nixon was quoted as saying. "His balls— his cojones."

With its heterosexual subtext, it was a typically phrased value judgment from Nixon, a man thought to be about as homophobic a president as we have ever had. But Annenberg was clearly of a more tolerant mind. In 1965 he hired interior designer William Haines, "Billy" to everyone in his lifetime, to decorate Sunnylands, and in 1969, he also hired him to do most of a million-dollar restoration of Winfield House, the U.S. ambassador's forty-room official residence in London. (In 1988 Annenberg sold his publishing empire, topped by *TV Guide*, to media mogul Rupert Murdoch for $3 billion. The ambassador died at ninety-four in 2002 and is survived by his wife, Leonore.)

And the point of all this? Billy Haines, who claimed he was born literally as midnight separated the nineteenth and twentiety centuries, for years had been known as one of the most "out" gay men in Hollywood. In fact, although his earlier film career is largely forgotten today (at least compared with those of Valentino and his ilk), Haines was immensely popular as a boy-next-door star of the silent-film era, sort of the Tab Hunter of his time. In 1925 he was MGM's top leading man, and from 1928 through 1932 Billy was never out of the list of the top five box office stars. (In 1930 he was America's number one film star.)

In *Sally, Irene, and Mary* (1925) he appeared with newcomers Joan Crawford and Constance Bennett, both of whom would play important roles in his future. His biggest successes also included that year's *Brown of Harvard*, a football saga with Jack Pickford (Mary's actor brother) and with John Wayne in an uncredited role as a Yale football player; *Little Annie Rooney* (1927), with Mary Pickford; and 1928's *Show People*, co-starring publisher William Randolph Hearst's famous mistress Marion Davies and directed by King Vidor. In 1928 Billy began his successful segue into sound in the part-talkie *Alias Jimmy Valentine,* and his first all-talkie, *Navy Blues,* was released the following year.

Nevertheless, only four years later, when MGM boss Louis B. Mayer found out under the worst possible circumstances that Haines was gay, he gave his leading "fegelah" (as he called homosexual men) the choice of entering into a sham marriage— they were then called "lavender marriages"—or staying with his lover of seven years, Jimmy Shields. Haines courageously (and unlike many other gay, lesbian, and bisexual actors of the era) chose to stay with Shields and was instantly fired (Mayer cast Robert Montgomery in upcoming Haines films). Unlike most studio executives of the era, Mayer was homophobic, but, Hollywood being Hollywood, he realized that homosexuals, both in front of as well as behind the camera, were vital to making movies. The reason he acted so violently was clearly because Haines' "outing"—by being caught *in flagrante delicto* with a young sailor at Los Angeles' downtown Y.M.C.A.—was very public and, in order to protect the studio's box office reputation, he had to do something drastic.

In any event, as the seventeenth-century British metaphysical poet George Herbert said, "Living well is the best revenge." And that's exactly what Billy did after he was fired.

After Haines made a few low-budget independent films with the backing of Marion Davies, he and Jimmy Shields opened an interior decorating firm. Immediately supported by former co-stars and friends such as Crawford, Lombard, Bennett, director George Cukor, and Gloria Swanson (who, long after the scandal was forgotten, offered him a part in *Sunset Boulevard,* which Haines declined), the business soon became the top decorating firm in Hollywood. It was Haines who created Crawford's trademark all-white decor; he had earlier co-starred with "Cranberry," as he nicknamed her (because of her hatred for her studio-picked name, which she said sounded like "crawfish"), in three silent films; including the previously mentioned *Sally, Irene, and Mary* and 1928's *West Point*. In it Billy played his signature wise-cracking young athletic type whose ego holds him back until he changes his attitude, leading in this case to a game-winning touchdown; next came 1929's *The Duke Steps Out*. For her part, Crawford adored Billy and called Haines and Shields "the happiest married couple in Hollywood. "Joan Crawford thought we should get married," Haines once recalled. "This was back in the 1920s, when I was a star and she was a rising flapper. It wasn't just a crass question of her ambition; we were very good but platonic friends. I told her, 'Cranberry (my pet name for her), that isn't how it works in Hollywood. They usually pair men who like men and ladies who like ladies.' Because if we both liked men, where would we be as man and wife, she'd resent me, and that would be the end of our beautiful friendship."

Speaking of George Cukor, Haines seems to have been the key to the puzzle of why Cukor was replaced by Victor Fleming as the original director of 1939's *Gone With the Wind*; it remains as the most famous directorial change in Hollywood history. Although some deny it, the story is that, years earlier, when Clark Gable, star of *Gone With the Wind*, was working as an extra in one of Haines' films, Cukor had a sexual encounter with the future superstar (he was said to have performed fellatio on Gable). Years later Gable, terrified that Haines may have told Cukor about it (in fact he had), demanded the director's replacement by a "man's director," that is, Fleming—Cukor was then famously recognized as "a woman's director" for his ability to work with superstar actresses such as Crawford, Katherine Hepburn, Lauren Bacall, and the like. The film's producer, David O. Selznick, himself frustrated over creative differences with Cukor, was said to be happy to accommodate his star despite protests from his leading lady, Vivian Leigh (whom, in fact, Cukor continued to coach throughout the making of the Civil War epic).

As we have seen, other than a few isolated cases of homophobia such as Mayer's, Hollywood at the time had basically
a live-and-let-live approach to homosexuality within the industry. Outside of the film industry, however, homosexuality was a
problem, driven, as we have seen, by box-office nervousness and
occasionally locally by the ongoing difficulty for relatively un-
sophisticated hopefuls to break into the movies for which many
blamed homosexuals in the industry. In 1936 Haines, Shields,
and their poodle (tinted purple for Easter) were at their beach
house in the El Porto neighborhood of Manhattan Beach. After a rumor circulated that Shields had molested a six-year-old
neighbor named Jimmy Walker, the son of a local businessman,
the pair were brutally beaten by members of the White Legion,
a Southern California version of the Ku Klux Klan. Joan Crawford, along with other stars such as Claudette Colbert, George
Burns, Gracie Allen, Kay Francis, and Charles Boyer, urged the
pair to report the assault to the police, and Marion Davies asked
her lover, William Randolph Hearst, to use his influence to make
sure that the perpetrators were prosecuted to the full extent of
the law. Ultimately Haines and Shields chose not to report the
incident because the event had already made enough headlines—
to their thinking—across America. No charges were ever filed
by Walker's parents either, because of lack of evidence.

In 1957 the pair bought a Palm Springs house in order to be
close to their many friends who had moved or retired to the desert,
filling it with their signature Chippendale and French furniture
and papering the walls with hand-painted Chinese wallpaper.
Among their local commissions was Jack and Ann Warner's
mansion in the Las Palmas neighborhood of Palm Springs and,
of course, Sunnylands. The Warners, for whom Haines had dec-
orated their 13,000-square-foot-plus mansion in Los Angeles,
were also frequent guests.

Ronald Reagan said in 1968 (when he was governor but thinking ahead to a run for the presidency) that homosexuality "was an abomination in the eyes of the Lord," and Nancy called it a "sickness." But, as with many other aspects of the homosexual experience in Hollywood, the reality was far different—at least for Nancy. For one thing, she never hesitated to be seen shopping with Haines and, when once asked if this was a problem for her, snapped "Not at all!" Nancy Reagan, in fact, had many gay friends (her godmother was the famed lesbian silent film star Alla Nazimova, who founded the legendary Hollywood hotel The Garden of Allah). "Billy had a wonderful sense of humor," she was quoted as saying in William Mann's biography of Haines, *Wisecracker*. "He had an elegance, a style [and] was a marvelous host," she added. " That style of living and entertaining has certainly disappeared. I certainly admired him."

Haines died from lung cancer and cardiac arrest at St. John's Hospital in Santa Monica, California, on December 26, 1973, while Jimmy sat by his bed. He was one week short of his seventy-third birthday. Three months later Shields, who suffered from what many now believe to be Alzheimer's disease, put on Haines' pajamas, took an overdose of pills, and crawled into their bed to die. "Goodbye to all of you who have tried so hard to comfort me in my loss of William Haines, who I have been with since 1926," read a note found next to his body. "I now find it impossible to go it alone—I am much too lonely."

Billy Haines' acting career lasted fourteen years. His decorating career lasted forty years. His relationship with Shields lasted forty-seven years.

They were cremated, and the urns holding their ashes reside side by side in the mausoleum at Santa Monica's Woodlawn Memorial Cemetery.

Billy and Jimmy may have had extracurricular affairs during their forty-seven years together, but they were hardly known within the industry as gay sexual exhibitionists. Not so director Edmund Goulding, whose major films included 1932's Best Picture Oscar-winner *Grand Hotel,* starring Greta Garbo, John and Lionel Barrymore, and Joan Crawford; the 1939 film *Dark Victory,* for which Bette Davis won the Best Actress Oscar; and the postwar existentialist drama *The Razor's Edge,* starring Tyrone Power and Gene Tierney. All are far better remembered than he is (he also directed the 1925 Billy Haines/Joan Crawford/Constance Bennett film *Sally, Irene, and Mary,* yet another example of how small a town—and industry—Hollywood was for decades).

In his time, besides being recognized as a highly adaptable director who also had ongoing drug and alcohol problems, Goulding was notorious for hosting bisexual orgies in both Los Angeles and at his three homes, owned successively, in Palm Springs. Art director George James Hopkins, whose film credits under both his and assumed names range from 1917's *Cleopatra* to 1975's *The Day of the Locust* (with such classics as *Casablanca, A Streetcar Named Desire, East of Eden, Auntie Mame,* and *Hello, Dolly!* in between), has recalled that attractive young men and women would be hired to have sex together, with Goulding directing their coupling as he would actors on a film set.

In 1932, when one of these parties went horribly wrong and two women participants ended up in the hospital, Goulding was told by his boss Louis B. Mayer to get out of the country. He was further ordered to stay away until Mayer, with the help of his lawyers and the then fairly corrupt Los Angeles Police Department, could cover up the scandal. When he eventually returned, Goulding made a couple of additional films at MGM, but he was then fired by Mayer, who, as we saw in the case of Billy Haines, despite his homophobia, could tolerate homosexuality so long as it didn't make news and embarrass the studio. Goulding then moved to Warner Brothers for ten years, and then to Twentieth Century Fox.

Goulding himself was gay, or certainly bisexual; biographer Matthew Kennedy claims Goulding was erotically attracted to men—he had several male lovers—but emotionally needed women. He was, in fact, married for three years to a dancer named Marjorie Moss, who died of tuberculosis in 1935.

•••••

Forgetting the orgies for a moment and considering the tremendous success of Goulding's films, one wonders why he is forgotten by so many film fans today. One reason, according to Kennedy, is that he was too adaptable and couldn't be pigeonholed; his thirty-seven films span too many genres, including heavy dramas, light comedies, and all-male action films. Since he doesn't have a strong identity in any one of them, he is not considered, to use a term that arrived with the 1950s, an "auteur" (the French word describing a film director whose films are so distinctive that he or she is perceived as a film's creator).

Then, too, he was also considered, like George Cukor, a "woman's director," which was, despite the quality of the films, considered some sort of lesser category of talent. The fact that he was also a multiple threat (he also wrote, cowrote or doctored some sixty scripts and plays, composed film music and in fact wrote songs and a musical), which confused the industry. (He also had a cameo in *Grand Hotel*.)

He bought his first place in Palm Springs in 1934 and soon added four guest cottages, among whose occupants at various times were David Niven—a friend despite Niven's homophobia, but understandable since, after a dozen or so films in Hollywood, it was Goulding's 1938 film *The Dawn Patrol* that made him a "star." Greta Garbo (a Goulding friend through thick and thin) and her then-lover, Mercedes de Acosta, also shared one of Goulding's cottages. So did the Countess Dorothy di Frasso (the American-born heiress who had earlier had an affair with Gary Cooper in Europe and introduced Cary Grant to Barbara Hutton, who would become his second wife), as well as tobacco heiress Doris Duke and also Mary Pickford. She and Niven were probably the only certifiably 100 percent straight people in the bunch.

Missing from the neighborhood was one of Goulding's best friends and lifelong champions, Joan Crawford. That's surprising, since Crawford acknowledged that it was by casting the actress in her second movie, 1925's silent *Sally, Irene, and Mary,* that he turned her "into an actress rather than a mere personality." In addition to the films already mentioned, Goulding embarked on a series of film projects any one or two of which would highlight any director's career. Among the earliest was 1927's *Love,* an adaptation of *Anna Karenina* starring Greta Garbo and John Gilbert, the era's celebrity couple who the year earlier had made their famous *Flesh and the Devil. Love* was quickly followed by one of the biggest scandals of the era, and the wreckage of the career of Gilbert, then Hollywood's highest paid matinee idol.

In September 1927, when Garbo and Gilbert were to be married (theirs was a relationship as passionately followed by film fans as Brad Pitt and Angelina Jolie's is today), Garbo famously stood him up, literally at the altar set up in William Randolph Hearst's Beverly Hills mansion, where the wedding and the party following were to be held (some blame Mercedes de Acosta's influence). Despite Garbo's no-show, Marion Davies, Hearst's movie star mistress, figured they might as well go on with the party (sans Garbo, of course) during which Gilbert's boss, Louis B. Mayer, said to his star: "What do you have to marry her for? Why don't you just screw her and forget about it?" Gilbert, who understandably had probably had a few too many drinks, flew into a rage and attacked and punched the magnate. Mayer shouted up from the floor, "You're finished, Gilbert. I'll destroy you if it costs me a million dollars."

Mayer kept his word and did his best to harm the actor, putting him into films of inferior quality, hurting his reputation, and warning other studios not to hire him. There is also a famous story that Mayer himself or his chief sound engineer manipulated the sound controls of Gilbert's first talkies so that his naturally high-pitched voice came out like a squeak; however it happened, when Gilbert declared "I love you, I love you, I love you" to Catherine Dale Owen in 1929's *His Glorious Night*, audiences throughout the country howled with laughter.

That year Goulding directed Gloria Swanson in *The Trespasser*, her first talkie, for which she received her second Best Actress Oscar nomination (her first Oscar was for *Sadie Thompson* the year before). Among Goulding's next films was *The Devil's Holiday* (1930), which also earned the popular Paramount star Nancy Carroll a Best Actress Oscar nomination, and 1934's *Riptide*, considered a minor film today but not then; its star was Norma Shearer, the so-called Queen of MGM and wife of the studio's "boy genius" production director, Irving Thalberg. The script was also one of several written by Goulding.

The year 1938 saw Goulding's aviation drama *The Dawn Patrol*, which did so much for David Niven's reputation (a remake of Howard Hawks' 1930 film, it also starred Errol Flynn and Basil Rathbone), and *The Old Maid* (1939), starring Bette Davis and Miriam Hopkins, still considered one of the best melodramas of the studios' golden era.

These were followed by 1941's *The Great Lie* in which Mary Astor steals the show from Bette Davis and won the Oscar for Best Supporting Actress (Goulding and Davis made four films together and locked horns on each of them); the romantic *The Constant Nymph* (1943), with Joan Fontaine pining for Charles Boyer (she was nominated for Best Actress but lost to Jennifer Jones for her performance in *The Song of Bernadette*), and *Claudia* (also in 1943), Dorothy McGuire's film debut.

The year 1946 brought *The Razor's Edge* (Clifton Webb and Ann Baxter were nominated for Best Supporting roles; Baxter won). *The Razor's Edge* starred Tyrone Power, who, despite three marriages, was bisexual. Power received the best reviews of his film career for his performance in Goulding's next film, the early noir *Nightmare Alley*. His co-star was Joan Blondell, who called Goulding "a nut" who insisted on acting out each scene before every take. Rounding out the constellation of Oscars won by actors in Goulding films, Edmund Gwenn won the Best Supporting Actor Oscar for his performance in the director's 1950 film *Mister 880*. In 1952 Goulding directed *We're Not Married!* a movie far more memorable for its cast than anything else; it included Ginger Rogers, Marilyn Monroe, Paul Douglas, Eve Arden, David Wayne, and Zsa Zsa Gabor.

Edmund Goulding was born in London on March 20, 1891, the son of a butcher. He started out on the stage as a child actor in 1903 and by 1909 was appearing on the West End in productions such as *Gentlemen, The King* and *Alice in Wonderland* (he played Alice). The year 1913 found him in a notorious production of Oscar Wilde's *The Picture of Dorian Gray*, adapted for the stage by G. Constant Lounsbery and produced by his friends following Wilde's scandalous fall from grace.

Goulding soon marched off to war but was invalided out of service because of a minor wound, and he was able to make his

New York stage debut in 1915. He then returned to the British army for the balance of the war, after which he came back to New York planning to be a singer, a plan he quickly dropped when he was commissioned to write screenplays for several early film stars; his greatest success was as coauthor of Henry King's *Tol'able David*, a 1921 silent masterpiece. In 1925 he joined the directing/screen writing pool at MGM and became a virtual overnight success with *Sally, Irene, and Mary*.

There followed the years when, seemingly, he could do no wrong, distinguished by brisk pacing and an ability to elicit honest emotion from his players. It couldn't last forever, and of course it didn't. At the end he was directing schlock like *Down Among the Sheltering Palms* and the Pat Boone musical *Mardi Gras*.

Edmund Goulding died on December 14, 1959, at the age of sixty-eight, reportedly during heart surgery at Cedars of Lebanon Hospital in Los Angeles. Some claim, however, that he actually committed suicide and the story of his dying during an operation was a cover-up.

# CHAPTER FOURTEEN

## MOSSY

On December 19, 1961, Moss Hart, one of America's greatest playwrights and directors who had retired to Palm Springs, went Christmas shopping on Palm Canyon Drive with his wife, the late Kitty Carlyle, their family, and actor Laurence Harvey (then just divorced from actress Margaret Leighton but known to friends to be gay, or certainly bisexual). The next morning Hart complained of a terrible toothache and, as Kitty was backing their car out of the garage of the house where they had lived for years to take him to the dentist, he collapsed on the lawn and died of a heart attack. Moss Hart was only fifty-seven.

He was also gay, although Kitty, an actress who became nationally famous as a regular on the long-running television quiz shows *To Tell the Truth* and *What's My Line* fiercely denied it during the marriage and throughout her long, forty-four-year widowhood (she died in 2007 at ninety-six years of age). He was also terribly conflicted over his sexual identity. It is even said that Kitty asked him if he was a homosexual before they mar-

ried in 1946; she later claimed he denied it. In her 1988 autobiography, *Kitty: An Autobiography*, she admits that her main career
when the pair were married was Moss Hart.

What this meant in practice was that during the marriage,
which lasted a little over fifteen years (1946–1961), Kitty basically stage-managed Moss's life. In the course of an oral history
interview with journalist Barbaralee Diamondstein that could
not be published during her lifetime, Kitty claimed that she had
not been in love with Moss when they married. Nor, she believed, was he in love with her. Both, she claimed, considered it
the right step at the right time and apparently figured that the
love part, if it came at all, might come later. Did it? They had
two children, Catherine and Christopher, but the two principals
aren't around to tell us any more.

One of the first things Kitty put a stop to were the all-boy
nude sunbathing parties around the pool at Hart's eighteenth-
century farmhouse home-away-from-home in Bucks County,
an upscale weekend haven near Philadelphia popular then and
now with show people (Hart's straight friend and collaborator George Kaufman had a nearby retreat as well). Apparently
Carlyle believed that although nothing could be changed about
what people knew of Moss's past, his life with her would be cir-
cumspect—and straight—or at least straight-appearing. It was
rumored that she even forbade him to see or associate with any
former friends and professional associates who were gay. When
she denied having said this in a 1992 *New Yorker* profile, at least
one of Moss's gay friends from his bachelor days called it a lie,
claiming that he had been banished on her orders after the marriage.

There seems little question that the reason Moss famously
spent years in therapy was because of guilt associated with his
attraction to men. In fact, in his screenplay for the 1952 film
*Hans Christian Andersen*, which starred the bisexual actor Danny

Kaye in the lead (Kaye's wife, Sylvia Fine, was famously as controlling of her husband's life as Kitty was of Hart's), Hart wrote a line for Kaye reading: "You'd be surprised how many kings are only a queen with a moustache."

In 1929 Hart wrote, and then rewrote with fellow playwright George Kaufman, *Once in a Lifetime,* a satire about a frustrated playwright in Hollywood, where the industry (and many careers) had recently been turned upside down by the arrival of sound. It was soon followed by several hit plays that established the team among the preeminent theatrical writers of the twentieth century. They included 1936's *You Can't Take It with You,* and *The Man Who Came to Dinner,* which debuted three years later. Though Kaufman had hits with others, Hart is generally conceded to be his most important collaborator.

*You Can't Take It with You,* the pair's most revived play, won the 1937 Pulitzer Prize. The following year a film version, directed by Frank Capra and starring James Stewart, Jean Arthur, Lionel Barrymore, Edward Arnold, Spring Byington, and Ann Miller, won both the Best Picture and Best Director awards.

•••••

*The Man Who Came to Dinner* features an obnoxious radio personality named Sheridan Whiteside who, after injuring himself slipping on ice, is forced to stay in a Midwestern family's house. Whiteside's character was based on the rotund critic and wit Alexander Woollcott, who was, with Kaufman, a founding member of the original Algonquin Round Table and a close friend of both Kaufman and Hart. Other characters in the play are based on Noel Coward, Harpo Marx, and Gertrude Lawrence.

Kaufman and Hart cowrote 1940's *George Washington Slept Here,* a comedy about a family who set about to restore a run-down farmhouse in Bucks County. A film version, also written by Kaufman and Hart and made in 1942, starred Jack Benny and Ann Sheridan. Then, Hart decided it was time to move on, and the partnership ended. This was not as dramatic a decision as theater gossip of the era claimed; throughout the preceding decade Hart had worked on his own on several musicals and revues, including *Face the Music* (1932), *As Thousands Cheer* the following year (with songs by Irving Berlin), and 1935's *Jubilee*, (his only collaboration with Cole Porter, whose songs for the show included "Begin the Beguine" and "Just One of Those Things." The cast included the fifteen-year-old (gay) future matinee idol Montgomery Clift. *Jubilee* was followed by 1937's *I'd Rather Be Right*, with music by Richard Rodgers and Lorenz Hart (not related to the playwright).

Hart continued his sensational career, writing, among other things, the book for the 1941 musical *Lady in the Dark* (songs by Kurt Weill and lyrics by Ira Gershwin) and such plays as 1948's *Light Up the Sky*, a somewhat dated comedy about the trials of opening a play on Broadway. All this while he was also emerging as a director, and it was for directing that he became best known during this period. In 1943, at the request of U.S. Army Air Force commander General Hap Arnold, Hart wrote the play *Winged Victory*. It was Hart's way of doing his part for the war effort, and it became one of the most successful morale builders of the war years. He certainly put himself into its creation, flying 28,000 miles by Air Force bomber to visit various installations (he hated flying), and sampling basic training under a fake name.

Waiving all royalties for a show that eventually grossed $10 million for the Army Emergency Relief, Hart wrote the show in less than a month and then, in only seventeen days, pared down over 7,000 performers to a still gigantic cast of 350 (the production company was actually classified as an official Army

Air Force base unit) and then staged it (the show also demanded seventy stagehands operating five revolving stages). It would go down in theatrical history as one of the biggest hits on Broadway, never to have a second production anywhere because of its size and expense. Some 350,000 people saw it during its Broadway run at the 44th Street Theater, and another 800,000 during a national tour.

The following year George Cukor, Hollywood's famously gay "woman's director," directed a film version of the play for Twentieth Century Fox. Its largely all-male military cast included many Hollywood stars then in uniform. Among them were Private First Class Edmond O'Brien, Private First Class Martin Ritt, Private Red Buttons (in drag, as an Andrews Sister), Staff Sergeant Peter Lind Hayes, Private Karl Malden, Private Barry Nelson, Sergeant Kevin McCarthy, Corporal Gary Merrill, Corporal Lee J. Cobb, future TV Superman Sergeant George Reeves, and Private Alfred Cocozza (alias Mario Lanza), augmented by the film debuts of Jeanne Crain and, in a small role, Judy Holliday.

A cast, they say, for the ages—a pity that not many people have seen it since its original, highly successful release in 1944. For years the release rights were tied up because of so many players; then after its premiere, the rights reverted to the Army (the air force was part of the army then). One wag has suggested that, if there is a print of the film somewhere out there, it is probably lying around in the Pentagon's basement.

Among the Broadway hits Hart directed during this time was *Junior Miss* in 1941, *Dear Ruth* (1944), and 1954's *Anniversary Waltz*. But by far the biggest directing hit of his career was to come in 1956: the musical *My Fair Lady*, with book and lyrics by Alan Jay Lerner and music by Frederick Loewe. The show, which ran on Broadway for seven years and spawned a hugely successful original cast album, won six Tony Awards, including Best Musical and, for Hart, Best Director. In 1964 it was made into a movie directed by George Cukor, with Audrey Hepburn replacing Julie Andrews, who created the part of Eliza Doolittle on Broadway.

Earlier Hart had already pulled off a show business hat trick by adding writing screenplays to his directing and playwriting laurels. Among the memorable films he wrote were 1947's *Gentleman's Agreement* (for which he received an Oscar nomination), *Hans Christian Andersen,* and the second version of *A Star Is Born,* with songs added for Judy Garland. (Moss and Kitty's desert neighbor, Janet Gaynor [Chapter 10], had played the Esther Blodgett/Vicki Lester character in the first version of the film, made in 1937.)

•••••

"I was born on Fifth Avenue," Moss Hart liked to say, according to a 1943 *Time* magazine feature. Then, as eyebrows went up, he added: "The wrong end!" It was Hart's humorous way of telling everyone how far he had come, but it wasn't true. He was born not on Fifth Avenue, but in a tenement at 74 East 105th Street on October 24, 1904. According to Steven Bach, author of *Dazzler,* the dazzling biography of Hart published in 1988, it was a neighborhood then defined by a huge immigrant population (Hart's family were English Jews), vendors with pushcarts, and New York Central trains shaking the buildings and filling the air with soot as they roared past.

Moss's father and maternal grandfather were cigar makers whose incomes eventually evaporated when automatic cigar-making machines came into common usage. The pair then began rolling cigars at the kitchen table in the tenement and selling them door-to-door.

Escape from grinding poverty came through his Aunt Kate, who, when he was very young, began taking him out of school on Thursdays to accompany her to theatrical matinees. Hart later called the trips "the beginning of a lifelong infection" with the stage. Sadly, the family lost contact with Kate in later years, and Hart even killed her off long before she actually died in his 1959 autobiography *Act One,* where he writes that she died in 1925 during the out-of-town tryouts for his teenage play *The Beloved Bandit.* The truth was, Aunt Kate suffered from a growing mental illness, which caused the falling out with his family; she wrote threatening letters, vandalized Hart's apartment, and, during rehearsals for *Jubilee* a decade later, actually was caught setting fires backstage at the Shubert theater.

But his relationship with Kate was life-forming, as Bach writes in *Dazzler,* and it also suggests a clue to his lifelong conflict over his sexual identity. Through his early exposure to theater—then America's most popular form of entertainment and Broadway the most glamorous address in the country—Bach says Moss discovered "the art of being somebody else…not a scrawny boy with bad teeth, a funny name…and a mother who was a distant drudge." So, apparently, Moss became that "somebody else" as far as his homosexuality was concerned and then spent a fortune with analysts when he discovered that doing so wasn't as easy as donning a costume.

Hart was forced to drop out of high school and take a job as a clothing folder at a garment factory to make ends meet. During that time he wrote what seems to be his first musical, a revue highlighting the company's clothing line. He also worked for a theatrical road show operator named Pitou, who paid him $15 a week but was so impressed with Hart's talent that he sank $45,000 in a musical that Hart wrote when he was nineteen called *The Beloved Bandit.* On the train from productions of *Bandit* in Rochester (New York) and Chicago, Hart shared a sleeper car with actor Gerald Griffen, who inscribed sheet music for the show: "To Mossy—who knows that the Garden of

Eden is not the one night stands or in a sleeper from Erie." Hart also spent time as an entertainment director for summer resorts along the Borscht Belt in the Catskills. He later said that keeping city folks sufficiently entertained when they are confronted with a few weeks of nature was the toughest job he ever had, but he learned a lot about drama from the experience, which he put to good use by writing his first Broadway hit. When the Kaufman–Hart show *Once in a Lifetime* proved to be a smash in 1929, Hart unabashedly began what his friends call "the gold garter period" of his life. There is a story that when money finally arrived, he and his family instantly deserted their Brooklyn tenement (to which they had moved from the upper East side tenement) without taking so much as a toothbrush and moved into a Manhattan apartment hotel. His new bedroom had four sets of curtains—net, chiffon, satin, velvet. Explained Hart: "I never had any curtains when I was poor, so I thought I'd like to have plenty."

As success topped success, *Time* magazine noted that the garters got golder and golder—by 1943 he had already banked more than a million dollars, the equivalent of twelve million or more today. Moss dressed like a dandy, had a town place, and owned a farm in Bucks County, Pennsylvania, where, besides having the swimming pool for the nude boys, he also planted thousands of pine trees, elm trees, and maples costing thousands of dollars; one visitor coined a phrase still popular today when he looked over Hart's spread and quipped, "It just goes to show you what God could do if He had money." Nevertheless, Hart was still so emotionally vulnerable—he suffered from nervous breakdowns dating from 1930—that he famously spent every opening night in the theater's men's room (presumably alone).

The last show Hart directed (he had to wait out the opening night in the men's room of the Majestic Theater) was the 1960 Lerner and Loewe musical *Camelot* based on the King Arthur legend. During a troubled out-of-town tryout in Toronto, Hart had a heart attack, and Kitty asked Lerner (who by then had a bleeding ulcer) to step in as director.

The show opened on December 3, 1960, before Hart was fully recovered, but he was well enough to rework the musical with Lerner (basically cutting the show's originally cumbersome length). The huge pre-opening ticket sales for the show and a cast performance on *The Ed Sullivan Show*, then one of the biggest shows on television, guaranteed that *Camelot* would be the hit we all know it became, running on Broadway for 873 performances, winning four Tony Awards, spawning several revivals and foreign productions, as well as a 1967 film version. The original-cast album was a top seller for over sixty weeks and was reportedly President John F. Kennedy's favorite bedtime listening. His favorite lines in the show were in the final number, in which Arthur knights a young boy and tells him to pass on the story of Camelot to future generations: "Don't let it be forgot, That once there was a spot, For one brief, shining moment, That was known as Camelot." It became, of course, indelibly associated with the Kennedy administration.

Moss Hart, as we know, didn't see all of this. He died a little over a year after the show opened. Kitty Carlisle wrote that she was devastated but went on living by Hart's precept that "you can't escape from life, you escape into it."

Sadly, at least as far as Moss Hart's private life was concerned, it didn't quite work out that way.

# CHAPTER FIFTEEN

# TRU AND GLORIA

*he Bad and the Beautiful* was a 1952 MGM film about a film producer who alienates everyone around him. Kirk Douglas played the producer and Lana Turner was Lorrison, a small-time actress who ends up a star—not quite the best metaphor for the stories related in this chapter, but close enough.

Not many people are aware that since 1992 Palm Springs has had its own version of the sidewalk stars that pave Hollywood's Walk of Fame. Many of them are along the city's main drag, Palm Canyon Drive, and originally—like the Hollywood stars— they were intended to celebrate the careers of stars who once lived or at least spent a lot of time in the desert resort. The city calls it The Walk of Stars.

And, indeed, many of the stars who became identified with the desert resort over the years are honored, among them actor William Powell (famed for his "Thin Man" series made between 1936 and 1947) and the former film and television star (and mayor) Charles Farrell (Chapter 10). There are stars commemorating Ruby Keeler, the tap-dancing star of several classic Warner Brothers musicals, who first visited Palm Springs with her husband, Al Jolson, in the late 1920s; Bob Hope; and Ginger Rogers, all of whom had homes in the area. (Rogers died at her Rancho Mirage place in April 1995.) But unlike Hollywood's stars, the honors tended to get out of hand on Palm Springs' sidewalks, and eventually the names of people you never heard of appear here and there among familiar names.

But the name of one former resident, one of the most talented and famous writers of the twentieth century, isn't there and probably never will be.

Fame, of course, has always had its downside, particularly in show business. Aging, changes in the public's taste, technological advances (particularly the switch from silent films—basically pantomime—to talkies in 1928), and even being publicly outed (as in the case of silent film star Billy Haines, Chapter 13), have all ended careers unless the individuals manage to reinvent themselves, as did, for example, teen heartthrob Tab Hunter (Chapter 8) once his halcyon days passed.

But few descents from fame are as poignant as that of Truman Capote's self-destruction after 1966. That year he was at the height of his once-considerable fame, during which the publication of his book *In Cold Blood* launched a new style of crime genre (the "factual novel"). And in November of that year he hosted his famous Black and White Ball at New York's Plaza Hotel, the social event of the season and probably of the generation.

Then, less than two years later, when he began spending a lot of time in Palm Springs—first renting then buying and renovating a house near the El Mirador resort (now the Desert Regional Hospital)—he very publicly began his precipitous fall into drugs and alcoholism.

Instead of writing his long promised next book, *Answered*

*Prayers*, in Palm Springs as he told everyone he would be doing, the writer, whose first novel, the semibiographical *Other Voices, Other Rooms* made him an instant celebrity at age twenty-four in 1948 (and world famous when his novella *Breakfast at Tiffany's* was published a decade later), did nothing. Days were spent with gossiping on the telephone beside his geranium-framed swimming pool, and nights with drinking heavily at dinner parties or local bars and clubs.

Perhaps the main reason for his not working on the book was tremendous ruckus that exploded when an excerpt from *Answered Prayers* titled "Le Cote Basque, 1965" was published in 1975 in *Esquire* magazine. In it, Capote violated an unwritten writers' code of friendship by quoting salacious lunch table conversation by several well-known socialites (and friends) at the then-fashionable restaurant. The women, among them his "best friend" Babe Paley (wife of CBS chairman William Paley, whom Capote also accused of cheating on his wife), Jacqueline Kennedy, and Gloria Vanderbilt, never spoke to him again. And one of the conversations, slightly fictionalized, claimed that the presumed accidental shotgun killing of her rich (possibly homosexual) husband William by former showgirl Ann Woodward years before was actually murder. Soon after it was published, Ann committed suicide by taking a cyanide pill (not before, as the tabloids gleefully reported, seeing to it that her makeup and hair were perfectly in place). Both of the couple's sons eventually committed suicide as well. As her mother-in-law later said (according to Susan Braudy in *This Crazy Thing Called Love*), "Well, that's that. She shot my son and Truman just murdered her and so now I suppose we won't have to worry about that anymore."

In all honesty, having that on one's conscience was probably enough to give anyone writer's block.

But to those Palm Springs dinner parties (hosted by the likes of Frank Sinatra, Bob Hope, and Walter and Leonore Annen-

berg at their celebrated Sunnylands estate) Capote would also
drag along his latest gay conquests, including local hustlers and,
in one notorious instance, an air-conditioning repairman from
Illinois. Now there is, of course, nothing wrong with having an
affair with a refrigerator repairman; the problem for Capote was
the outraged response it engendered among the elite friends who
invited him. To them, it spelled social death in the Palm Springs
of the era.

Truman was misbehaving in other ways as well. The young
writer Joseph Wambaugh and his wife, Dee, visited him for a
weekend in about 1971. Dwight Garner, writing in the *New York
Times* Sunday Book Review in April 2008, notes that Wambaugh
claimed that during that visit, while he was telling Capote the
story of his planned *The Onion Field* book, Capote arranged mat-
ters so that he would be alone with the "then-cute-and-young"
cop by knocking Dee unconscious with a drugged vodka Screw-
driver. To this day, Garner says, Wambaugh's wife claims that Capote indeed slipped her the mickey, adding nevertheless that she is
probably the only woman ever to have slept in Capote's bed.

As was earlier mentioned, one of the reasons cited for the
popularity of Palm Springs among gays and lesbians are the
privacy-providing walls, and Capote's house had (and still has)
walls so high that all you can see from inside are the mountain
peaks and the tops of nearby palm trees. There he could play
with his bulldog, Charlie, and lounge around his pool. He could
also entertain as he wished; his guest the same weekend that the
Wambaughs visited was a bartender from Manhattan's Studio
54—his home was then also a haven for drug dealing—whom he
also squired around to society parties in the city.

He also loved being pampered at the nearby Palm Springs
Spa (oddly, Capote hated the Racquet Club, which for years had
been the city's ground zero for gossip). And, of all things, he
also loved ice skating, usually alone, at the long-gone Palm Des-

ert Ice Skating Center, where, outfitted in a space age outfit by the French designer Andre Courreges ("Lots and lots of zippers," Capote would often laugh), where he did solo spins in the "blue gloom" of the skating rink.

In 1974 Capote was admitted to the Eisenhower Medical Center in nearby Rancho Mirage, suffering from, it was claimed at the time, "exhaustion." He was later hospitalized at the Eisenhower four times in 1981, seven times in 1982, and sixteen times the following year for alcohol-related illnesses.

After returning to Los Angeles from a trip to Key West, Capote died while staying at the home of Joanne Carson (Johnny's second wife) on August 25, 1984. The coroner reported that he did not die directly from a drug overdose, as was largely speculated at the time, but from "liver disease complicated by phlebitis and multiple drug intoxication." There was no alcohol found in his system and the drug levels, "although contributory, were not lethal and indicated regular usage with his past medical history."

Shortly before his death Capote told Joanne that he had finally finished *Answered Prayers* and was preparing to die in peace; she allegedly had read three chapters prior to his death and described them as being "very long." Other friends also claimed he had read the missing chapters from the book to them but admitted he may have been improvising.

On the morning preceding his death, Capote gave Carson a key to a safe deposit box that he said contained the completed novel, but he wouldn't tell her where the locker was located. "The novel will be found when it wants to be found," were among the writer's last words. After his death, there was an exhaustive search for the manuscript in cities where Capote hinted it might be located, but nothing was ever found.

*Answered Prayers*, however, was published in an unfinished form in 1987.

Gloria Greene, like Capote, was a homosexual. And like Capote, she was a hard drinker. Unlike Truman Capote, she was relatively unknown to the world at large, but for part of a generation she was a famous host and de facto philanthropist in the city. And, unlike Capote, her memory is celebrated by one of Palm Springs' Walk of Stars. Her story, unlike that of Capote's, is an example of much that is good about the contributions of gay and, in Greene's case, lesbian contributions to the city's image today.

Although the name and memory of Ms. Greene have receded somewhat since her death in the late 1990s, there are many—mostly longtime residents—who remember her as one of the city's most benevolent characters and host of several of the community's most popular gay and lesbian restaurants and bars. She is also remembered as one who did something about the AIDS plague when she and her (straight) friend, the late Jeannette Rockefeller (widow of Winthrop Rockefeller and former first lady of Arkansas) cofounded the AIDS Awareness Project, which today, supported by private contributions, feeds 500 or more low-income area residents suffering from HIV/AIDS.

Like Lois Kellogg (Chapter 3), Gloria came from Chicago. And like several of Kellogg's friends in the early days of Palm Springs, including Dr. Florilla White and her sister Cornelia, she was rarely seen in a dress, adopting from the beginning a trademark outfit of blue denim jeans, an open blue denim shirt, and a cowboy hat. She was an outdoor gal, tanned as deeply as walnut, seemingly always with a cigarillo in her mouth, and possessing an unforgettable gravelly voice. And, at a time when the "establishment" ran the city, she openly catered to the city's gay and lesbian population, first by opening His and Hers bar and restaurant in nearby Cathedral City. As was noted earlier, Palm

Springs wouldn't allow such operations until later, when she then opened what would be the city's first gay and lesbian restaurant and bar, Gloria's. It was also followed by Gloria's opening of other gay enterprises including the Palm Canyon Inn.

Gloria's in its time was so popular that it was also a destination for heterosexuals; the Reverend Andrew Green, the rector of St. Paul in the Desert Episcopal Church, recalls that his first meal in Palm Springs when he arrived nineteen years ago was lunch at Gloria's at the invitation of a gay member of his new church. It also had a cachet that few other restaurants and bars in Palm Springs enjoyed. John Hartshorn, who is now a resident of Denver but for the decade of the 1980s lived in Palm Springs, recalls that the first time he walked into Gloria's, he responded to the ambiance of the place by saying, "I could be a star here!" Also, like the Chi-Chi club nearby, Gloria's attracted its own set of stars, including Ruby Keeler. If Gloria's had been around a decade or two earlier, Greta Garbo would have probably stopped by if she was certain she would be left alone; reportedly Greene and she had once been lovers.

Resident Bill Jones first met Gloria in 1984, soon after he began vacationing in the city and a decade before he decided to live full-time and operate his multi-branch, forty-year-old Carousel Catering company in Palm Springs. "We were very good friends," he recalls. "She was a lot of fun to be around, had a great love for people, and a positive attitude. She was convinced that, whatever the problem, everything would always come out ok…a really good egg."

When the AIDS crisis arrived in force in Palm Springs, Gloria started feeding victims out of the back door of her restaurant; she was following her belief that yes, you can live better with the medicines, but if you don't have proper nutrition and healthy food, you're not going to have quality of life. "My philosophy has always been to make a little from a lot," Greene told journalist Jim Quinlin in 1997. "And by generating just a few dollars from a whole lot of people, we [came] up with sufficient funds for the AIDS Assistance Program. From where I sit, feeding the hungry should be easy—effortless! Who can sit by and watch anyone starve?"

When Truman Capote, who left a middling amount of tremendously good work, died, the news was treated as a major news story in media across the world. When Gloria Greene, who left a legacy of equally good, but far different work, died, the Palm Springs newspaper, the *Desert Sun*, apparently, didn't even bother with an obituary.

*Sic transit Gloria mundi*...well, paraphrasing the Latin, "thus passes a glory of Palm Springs."

But in her lifetime of hospitality and service, Gloria Greene did as much as any star or celebrity to make Palm Springs the gay and lesbian oasis it is today.

# BIBLIOGRAPHY

Allen, Frederick Lewis. *Since Yesterday, 1929-1939*. Bantam, 1940.

Anderson, Clinton A. *Hollywood Is My Beat*. Prentice Hall, 1960.

Anger, Kenneth. *Hollywood Babylon*. Self-published (Associated Professional Services, Phoenix, AZ), 1965.

Auden, W. H. *Forewords and Afterwords*. Vintage, 1990.

Bainbridge, John. *Garbo*. Holt, Rinehart & Winston. 1951.

Beauchamp, Cari. *Without Lying Down*. University of California Press, 1997.

Berg, A. Scott. *Kate Remembered*. G. P. Putnam's Sons, 2003.

Bogert, Frank. *Palm Springs: First Hundred Years*. Palm Springs Heritage Associates, 1987.

Burk, Margaret, and Hudson, Gary. *Final Curtain*. Seven Locks Press. 1996.

Callow, Simon. *Charles Laughton: A Difficult Actor*. Grove/Atlantic, 1988.

Chase, J. Smeaton. *Our Araby: Palm Springs and the Garden of the Sun*. 1920. Reprinted: Palm Springs Public Library. Chronicle Books, 2001.

Clarke, Gerald. *Capote, A Biography*. Simon & Schuster, 1988.

Danish, Andrew. *Palm Springs Weekend: The Architecture and Design of a Midcentury Oasis*. Chronicle Books, 2001.

Davie, Michael. *California, the Vanishing Dream*. Dodd, Mead, 1972.

Davies, Marion. *The Times We Had.* Ballentine, 1975.

DeMille, C. B. *Autobiography.* Prentice-Hall, 1951.

Duncan, Paul. *Cary Grant.* Taschen Books, 2007.

Esquevin, Christian. *Adrian: Silver Screen to Custom Label.* Monacelli, 2008.

Finch, Christopher & Rosenkranz, Linda. *Gone Hollywood.* Doubleday, 1979.

Friedrich, Otto. *City of Nets.* University of California Press. 1986.

Gebhard, David, and von Breton, Harriette. *Los Angeles in the Thirties.* Hennessey+Ingalls, 1989.

Goodman, Ezra. *The Fifty Year Decline and Fall of Hollywood.* Simon & Schuster, 1961.

Graham, Sheilah. *Confessions of a Hollywood Columnist.* Wm. Morrow, 1969.

Hadleigh, Boze. *Hollywood Gays.* Barricade, 1996.

Higham, Charles. *C. B. DeMille.* Scribners. 1973.

———. *Charles Laughton: An Intimate Biography.* Doubleday, 1976.

Higham, Charles and Moseley, Roy. *Cary Grant: The Lonely Heart.* Harcourt, Brace, Jovanovich, 1989.

Hopper, Hedda. *From Under My Hat.* Macfadden, 1963.

Hunter, Tab. *Tab Hunter Confidential.* Algonquin Books of Chapel Hill, 2005.

Isherwood, Christopher. *Christopher and His Kind, 1929-1939.* Farrar, Straus, & Giroux, 1976.

———. *Diaries, 1939-1960.* HarperCollins, 1996.

———. *Lost Years: A Memoir 1945-1951.* HarperCollins, 2000.

Jacobson, Laurie. *Hollywood Heartbreak.* Fireside/Simon & Schuster, 1984.

———. *Dishing Hollywood: The Real Scoop on Tinseltown's Most Notorious Scandals.* Cumberland House, 2003.

Johannson, Warren, and Percy, William A. *Outing: Shattering the Conspiracy of Silence.* Harrington Park Press, 1994.

Johns, Howard. *Palm Springs Confidential.* Barricade Books, 2004.

Johnson, Paul. *Modern Times: The World from the Twenties to the Eighties.* Harper Row, 1983.

Kanin, Garson. *Moviola.* Pocket Books, 1979.

Lanchester, Elsa. *Elsa Lanchester, Herself.* St. Martin's Press, 1983.

Loos, Anita. *Kiss Hollywood Good-bye.* Viking, 1974.

Madsen. Axel. *The Sewing Circle.* Birch Lane Press, 1995.

Mann, William J. *Wisecracker: The Life and Times of William Haines, Hollywood's First Gay Star.* Penguin, 1998.

———. *Behind the Screen: How Gays and Lesbians Shaped Hollywood, 1910-1969.* Viking, 2001.

Martin, Mary. *My Heart Belongs.* William Morrow & Co., 1976.

McCann, Graham. *Cary Grant.* Columbia University Press, 1998.

McClellan, Diana. *The Girls.* LA Weekly Books/St. Martin's Press, 2000.

McGilligan, Patrick. *Alfred Hitchcock: A Life in Darkness and Light.* New York, New York: Regan Books. 2003.

Merrill-Mirsky, Carol. *Exiles in Paradise.* Catalog of the Hollywood Bowl Museum exhibition of the same name. Navigator Press, 1991.

Niemann, Greg. *Palm Springs Legends.* Sunbelt Publications, 2006.

Parish, James Robert. *Hollywood's Great Love Teams.* New Rochelle, N.Y., Rainbow Books, 1978.

Rogers St. Johns, Adela. *Love, Laughter and Tears: My Hollywood Story.* Doubleday, 1978.

Ronald L. Davis. *Mary Martin, Broadway Legend.* University of Oklahoma Press, 2008.

Russo, Vito. *The Celluloid Closet: Homosexuality in the Movies.* Harper and Row, 1987.

Schatz, Thomas. *The Genius of the System: Hollywood Filmmaking in the Studio Era.* Metro/Henry Holt, 1988.

Silvester, Christopher (editor). *Hollywood.* Grove Press. 1998.

Spoto, Daniel. *The Dark Side of Genius: The Life of Alfred Hitchcock.* Da Capo Press, 1999.

———. *Laurence Olivier: A Biography.* Cooper Square Press. 2001.

Starr, Kevin. *Inventing the Dream.* Oxford University Press, 1985.

———. *Material Dreams.* Oxford University Press, 1990.

Thomson, David. *Beneath Mulholland: Thoughts on Hollywood and Its Ghosts,* Vintage, 1997.

Tillmany, Jack and Dowling, Jennifer. *The Theatres of Oakland.* Arcadia Publishing, 2006.

Torrence, Bruce T. *Hollywood: The First Hundred Years.* New York Zoetrope, 1982.

Vieira, Mark A. *Greta Garbo: A Cinematic Legacy*, Abrams, 2006.

Wallace, David. *Lost Hollywood.* St. Martin's, 2000.

———. *Hollywoodland.* St. Martin's, 2002.

———. *Malibu, A Century of Living by the Sea* (Foreword). Abrams, 2005.

———. *Dream Palaces of Hollywood's Golden Age.* Abrams, 2006.

———. *Exiles in Hollywood.* Limelight, 2006.

Wilson, Edmund. *The Twenties.* Farrar, Straus, & Giroux, 1979.

———. *The Thirties.* Farrar, Straus, & Giroux, 1980.


Additional material was drawn from historic periodicals, including:

*Modern Screen*

*Motion Picture*

*Photoplay*

*Silver Screen, Confidential.*

# INDEX

Green, Andrew, Rev., 30-32, 179
Green, Christopher, 23
Greene, Gloria, 11, 26, 30, 32, 178-80
Gregory, Paul, 122
Griffen, Gerald, 169
Gustafson, Sven, 82
Gwenn, Edmund, 161

Hagman, Benjamin J., 131
Hagman, Lawrence M., 131-32, 135, 137
Haines, William, 16, 124-25, 152-57, 174
Hall, Peter, 148
Halliday, Mary H., 134
Halliday, Richard, 129, 133-34, 136-37
Hammerstein II, Oscar, 129, 134, 136
Harding, Laura, 80
Harlow, Jean, 119
Harris, Jennifer, 58
Harris, Julie, 101
Harrison, Rex, 77
Hart, Catherine, 164
Hart, Christopher, 164
Hart, Kate, 169
Hart, Kitty Carlyle, 163-65, 168, 171
Hart, Lorenz, 135, 166
Hart, Moss, 163ñ71
Harvey, Joan, 97
Harvey, Laurence, 97, 163
Hauser, Gayelord, 82
Hawks, Howard, 160
Hawn, Goldie, 140
Hayes, Helen, 135
Hayes, Peter Lind, 167
Hayward, Louis, 145
Head, Murray, 147
Hearst, William Randolph, 61, 152, 155, 159

Heflin, Van, 103
Hemingway, Ernest, 80, 89
Hemming, Stefan, 107, 114
Hemmings, David, 104
Hepburn, Audrey, 167
Hepburn, Katherine, 18, 75, 77, 80, 121, 154
Herbert, George, 153
Herlihy, John, 146
Herman, Woody, 133
Heston, Charlton, 89
Hewitt, Edgar Lee, 36
Heymann, C. David, 120
Hicks, Alvah, 113
Hitchcock, Alfred, 19, 52, 95
Hodges, Ken, 88
Hoffman, Dustin, 146-47, 149
Holliday, Judy, 80, 167
Hope, Bob, 151, 174-5
Hopkins, George James, 157
Hopkins, Miriam, 160
Hopper, Hedda, 78-79
Horn, Frank, 53
Hudson, Doug, 24-27
Hudson, Rock, 18, 75, 84-89, 90, 92-94, 98, 101, 108-09
Hughes, Howard, 57
Hugo, Victor, 126
Hunter, Jeffrey, 148
Hunter, Ross, 68
Hunter, Tab, 18-9, 67, 84-85, 95, 98-105, 107-08, 152-74
Hutcheson, Rick, 24
Hutton, Barbara, 53, 56-57, 159

Ince, Thomas, 120
Ivano, Paul, 41-2

Jackman, Hugh, 148
Jackson, Glenda, 147
Jackson, Helen Hunt, 34

James I, King of England, 14
James, George Wharton, 33
Jesus, 14
Johns, Howard, 31, 114
Jolie, Angelina, 159
Jolson, Al, 40, 174
Jones, Bill, 179
Jones, Jennifer, 160

Kabotie, 37
Karloff, Boris (William Henry Pratt),
  141-42, 144, 148
Kaufman, George, 164-66, 170
Kaufmann, Edgar, 25
Kaye, Danny, 17-8, 164-65
Keats, John, 12
Keeler, Ruby, 174, 179
Kellogg, Lois, 45-9, 50-51, 178
Kelm, Arthur (Tab Hunter), 100
Kelm, Charles, 100
Kennedy, Jacqueline, 175
Kennedy, John F., President, 171
King, Henry, 161
Kirkwood, James, 137
Krueger, Paul, 75, 124

Lake, Veronica, 79
Lamarr, Hedy, 92
Lancaster, Burt, 80
Lanchester, Elsa, 18, 141, 144
Lanza, Mario (Alfred Cocozza), 167
Laughton, Charles, 18, 140-41
Lawrence, Gertrude, 165
Lee, Gypsy Rose, 132
Leigh, Janet, 91
Leigh, Vivien, 17-18, 154
Lerner, Alan J., 167, 170
LeRoy, Josh, 66
LeRoy, Mervyn, 67
Levis, Jessica, 35
Lewis, David, 145

Liberace, 25, 83, 107-17
Liberace, Dora, 116
Liberace, George, 107, 114
Livingston, Margaret, 120-21
Lloyd, Harold, Jr., 97
Loewe, Frederick, 167, 170
Lombard, Carole, 54, 120, 153
Loren, Sophia, 12,
Lounsbery, G. Constant, 161
Lubo, Ramona, 34
Lugosi, Bela, 142

MacLaine, Shirley, 102, 148
MacMurray, Fred, 77
Madison, Guy, 84
Malden, Karl, 167
Malone, Dorothy, 101, 108
Manilow, Barry, 24
Mankiewicz, Joseph L., 78
Mann, William J., 53, 120, 124, 158
Manson, Charles, 57
March, Frederic, 67, 77
Margaret, Princess, 151
Marlowe, Scott, 95
Martin, Mary, 117-18, 120, 122,
  129-37
Martin, Tony, 91
Marx, Harpo, 165
Marx, Zeppo, 67
Matlin, Marlee, 118
May, Clarence, 81
Mayer, Louis B., 80,103, 113, 153,
  155, 157, 159-60
McCallum, John, 38, 49
McCarthy, Senator Joe, 73
McCarthy, Kevin, 167
McGrath, Pat, 31
McGuire, Dorothy, 161
McKellan, Ian, Sir, 139
McKesson, William B., 70
Mellen, Bob, 29, 31-2
Merman, Ethel, 135